P9-DWV-943

Mining Camp Days

Mining Camp Days

Bodie • Aurora • Bridgeport • Hawthorne
Tonopah • Lundy • Masonic • Benton
Thorne • Mono Mills • Mammoth
Sodaville • Goldfield

By EMIL W. BILLEB

NEVADA PUBLICATIONS

© Copyright 1968 by Howell-North Books, a corporation, all rights reserved. Copyright transferred to Stanley
W. Paher in 1985. No part of this book may be
reproduced in any manner without permission in writing,
except in the case of brief quotations embodied in critical
articles and reviews.

Proudly printed in the United States of America
ISBN 0-913814-05-9

1986 Edition

ublished by Stanley Paher
Nevada Publications
Box 15444
Las Vegas, Nev. 89114

FOREWORD

From the historian's point of view, this volume is a triumph of good judgment: Emil Billeb's in writing it around the bonanza of illustrative material he has gathered during the years; the publisher's in recognizing the value of this first-hand account of the Great Basin's twentieth century boom camps and mining operations, a colorful but much neglected era of Western history.

Here is history at its most attractive, seen through the observant eye of a fastidious reporter, photographer and participant. Bodie, Tonopah, Goldfield, Thorne, Mono Mills, Aurora, Benton, Bridgeport, Lundy and Broken Hills come alive from the grayness of six decades, or even less, and the reader joins Emil Billeb and his fellow argonauts in a swirl of mining stocks, kited checks, claim jumping, mine promotions and cantankerous railroading that caught and held their fancy.

His personal odyssey began on Wall Street and ranged through boom town after boom town to San Francisco. Even as this is written, he is once again romancing with his first love, mining. His other loves are set forth in the pages that follow. This is more than just a personal recollection; it is the saga of one of the Far West's finest gentlemen who finally tells his story after living four score years of history, which he was able to recognize even as it happened. His sense of the dramatic led him nearly always to keep a camera nearby, ready for the unusual or unexpected. He still does this.

As a long-time friend of Emil Billeb, I am happy that his story is now recounted in this treasure of a book. It will be prized by those who have known or heard of him or the Cain family or the Bodie & Benton Railroad or Mono County or Nye

County. Those who meet them for the first time in these pages will find this a heartwarming handshake with a past that is not too distant, after all.

Some of the stopes have caved; some of the towns have wasted away to nothing; most of the rails have rusted; and the stamp mills are silent. Still, with Emil Billeb, we can revisit this land of heady opportunity and catch some of the glow that was caught before and which will surely, some day, be caught again by the likes of you and me.

DONALD I. SEGERSTROM

Sonora, California
March 23, 1968

PREFACE

It was with some hesitation that I embarked on the writing of this book, but I succumbed to the urging of my family and many friends, especially Mr. Donald I. Segerstrom of Sonora, California. This is the story of my life in the mining camps of Nevada and eastern California after 1905, especially during the boom days of Tonopah, the waning years of Aurora, and—wildest of them all—Bodie where I was employed from 1908 until 1920.

I then moved to San Francisco but continued my interest in the mining districts east of the Sierra. Since retiring in 1950, I have been particularly interested in preserving Bodie for future generations. I represented the J. S. Cain Co., owners of much of the old town, in negotiations with the State of California which at last, to my deep satisfaction, resulted in creation of the Bodie State Historical Park. I greatly appreciate the aid and encouragement of others in this effort, particularly Mr. Segerstrom, John N. Rosekrans of San Francisco, Dr. V. Aubrey Neasham of Sacramento and Senator Paul J. Lunardi, Mono County's representative in the Legislature.

This book is a further effort, in another medium, to preserve some of the flavor of life in the mining camps. The stories are all true and told as I remember them, except that prudence has sometimes led me to disguise the name of a participant.

EMIL W. BILLEB

San Francisco
April, 1968

To the memory of my wife,
and to my sons —
all of them children of Bodie.

TABLE OF CONTENTS

Pacific Coast Borax Company,

100 William Street.

Borax.
Boric Acid.
Borax Soaps.
Boric Preparations.

C. B. Zabriskie,
Eastern Manager.

New York, Sept. 20, 1905.

Mr. Emil W. Billeb,

157 West 103rd St., City.

My dear friend:

Enclosed find letters of introduction to three very dear friends of mine who are influential men in the section of the country to which you are going and can be of assistance to you.

I sincerely hope that you will be successful when you get out there, and if after you get there, there is anyone else you think I could write to to help you just let me know.   You are going to a very active section of the country where everything is just at its beginning and if you go with the determination of taking whatever position offers itself and doing that work with the best of your ability, it will certainly lead to other and better positions and your ultimate success.   This, I feel sure, you are prepared to do.

With my very best wishes, believe me,

Yours very truly,

C.B.Z.-E.

CHAPTER ONE

BOOMING TONOPAH

i. *How it all began*

It all began, I am told, when I was born in Cologne, Germany, the third son and fourth child of Ernst A. Billeb and Bertha Bücklers Billeb, both German-born. I have few memories of my early years in Germany or of the family's move to New York aboard the steamship *Elbe*. My parents settled the family in a typical brownstone residence on 46th Street between Sixth Avenue and Broadway, then a good residential district. While we lived there, my younger sister was born.

I attended public schools in New York and Brooklyn and also Pratt Institute for a Saturday art course. After finishing in the public schools I took a position as junior clerk in the law firm of Man & Man in Wall Street. The four Man brothers represented many prominent estates and did business with many banks and trust companies. I considered taking up the study of law, but in the meantime went to night school for courses in accounting and typewriting.

In my travels about the financial district for the firm, I had the opportunity of seeing many prominent figures of the financial world, including Hetty Green and J. P. Morgan, the elder. I also became acquainted with Mr. and Mrs. Christian B. Zabriskie. He was general manager of the Pacific Coast Borax Co. with offices in New York, a company controlled by the "Borax King," F. M. Smith. Natives of the West, the Zabriskies had been residents of the mining camp of Candelaria, Nevada, not far from the California boundary. Here they met Smith, who lived there before he embarked on his highly successful borax business. Later they were interested in the development of Tonopah and other Nevada mining camps.

During the summer of 1905 I had several discussions with Mr. Zabriskie about Tonopah and its possibilities. On one occasion, talking with my brother Gus (August F. Billeb) and myself, he said, "If I were a young man I would go to Tonopah." This settled the matter for Gus and me.

This, in brief, is the background of my family and the circumstances which led to our decision to go west. My father had died some years previously. My oldest brother had already embarked on a venture which eventually settled him in India. My mother and sisters continued to make their home in New York. Gus and I boarded the transcontinental train for Nevada.

ii. Off to Nevada

October 7, 1905 was a momentous day for us as we pulled up our roots in New York City and headed west for Tonopah. It was quite a jump at that time for two young tenderfeet who had never been west of New York State, especially to go to a booming Nevada mining camp. We had a couple of letters of introduction to friends of the Zabriskies to give us some confidence.

Our trip west by train, in an upper berth, was via Chicago, Omaha and Reno. As the train approached Hazen, Nevada, a gentleman in our car approached us and asked our destination. We told him it was Tonopah and he said that the conductor might suggest that we get off at Hazen where a connection could now be made for Tonopah and the southern Nevada camps, instead of going on to Reno 45 miles further west. At that time Hazen was just a construction camp in the desert and the man told us it was a rough and unsafe place for our layover while waiting for the Tonopah train the following day. Perhaps, from our attire, he sized us up as being "greenhorns" and ready for plucking. We thanked him and told the conductor we would continue on to Reno as our tickets provided.

At Reno we secured a room in the Overland Hotel near the station. It proved a noisy place with trains coming and going all night, to and from the West Coast. The city was booming and crowded with people from all directions, either coming from or going to the gold fields of southern Nevada. At the time, Reno's population did not exceed 7500 and in all of Nevada there were no more than 80,000 people. The first thing that impressed us there was the wide-open gambling with five-, ten- and twenty-dollar gold pieces stacked up like the silver dollars of recent memory. As yet there were none of the slot machines as we know them and penny gambling did not exist.

The buildings of the business district were mostly three or four stories high and people were clothed in attire ranging from cowboy and miners' outfits to the more sedate suits of the business people. All this contrasted sharply with our New York styles.

The daylight trip from Reno to Tonopah was on the Southern Pacific back east to Hazen, then south over desert country, often varied by small settlements with ranches, green trees and vegetation. The train passed Fort Churchill, a historic military post of earlier days, Wabuska, Yerington, Schurz, Walker Lake and Thorne, the station for Hawthorne. At Mina the new Tonopah Railroad took over, passing through Sodaville, Coaldale and on to Tonopah, where we arrived that evening, October 12, 1905.

iii. Impressions of Tonopah

Seeking accommodations for the night, we managed to get a room with double bed in the Merchants Hotel on Main Street. During the night the wind was blowing in hard gusts and we noticed the ceiling of our room billowing up and down with each gust. On examination, we found that it was made of light cloth to which wallpaper had been pasted; with no solid backing this ceiling was easily pushed up and down by the wind. Such shoddy construction was quite common in the mushrooming boom towns of Nevada.

Our first tour of inspection in Tonopah was to find a place where we could live on our meager funds. Presently we found a room in a recently constructed building not far from the center of town, where for forty dollars a month, paid in advance, we were provided with a double bed, dresser, two chairs and a sheet iron stove. We were assisted in finding this room by a new-found friend, an attorney named Fred Berry who later became well known in San Francisco. We were soon settled with our two suitcases and set out to get our bearings.

Tonopah was a busy place, mines going full blast and streets crowded with people and traffic. No automobiles were in evidence, but the wide north-and-south Main street, formerly known as Sawtooth Pass, was thronged with people, teams and wagons of all sorts.

We were impressed with the jerk-line teams, some with twenty horses and mules pulling trains of heavily loaded wagons, generally two large freight wagons and a smaller feed wagon to which the animals were tied at night. In many instances water barrels were mounted on the side of the freight schooner for use when making a dry camp on the desert. The teams were harnessed in pairs, attached to a long chain extending from the first wagon to the lead horses or mules. The teamster sat in a saddle on the "near" or left wheel horse and controlled the team by a jerk-line leading to the bridles of the lead team. The lead animals had to move together as they were connected by a light rod. It was quite a sight to see the teamster's handling of the teams on the rough and sometimes crooked roads. The teams generally averaged close to a ton of freight per animal. Ten to fifteen miles per day was considered a good speed.

East of town and on the slopes of Mount Oddie were many prosperous mines, including the Mizpah, site of Jim Butler's discovery that resulted in the Tonopah boom. This was one of the first places we went to visit, wearing our elegant New York derby hats.

While we were standing in front of the mine works, looking out over the town to the west, someone came up behind me and pushed my hat over my eyes. When I removed my crushed derby, there was a tall young fellow standing by me with a wide grin on his face. He introduced himself as Joe Nelson, from Nelson, California, said he was another recent arrival and looking for work. He told me he could not resist the temptation to bang down on that hat, which he assured us was not the thing for a young fellow to wear in Nevada, particularly right by a mine. We threw away our New York hats and went back to town to get more appropriate headgear.

iv. Our bachelor household

When the first month's rent on our room was up, we joined forces with Joe Nelson and two other young fellows from the East, John M. Peters and Jack Roach. The five of us rented a building on the west side of town that had a couple of bedrooms and a kitchen. We took turns at the cooking, dishwashing and housework. The arrangement worked out well except for one thing: I had the only key to the house, locked up in the morning and was usually the first to arrive in the evening to unlock the door. A couple of times I arrived late, and found the others waiting for me to open the door. The second time this happened, I unlocked the door and we threw the key out in the sagebrush. From then on the house remained unlocked. While Tonopah had its brawls and rough people, we never knew anyone to go into our house or molest a thing.

Food prices were fairly high; so were wages for those days. The lowest was four dollars a day for common surface labor; higher rates prevailed depending on the type of work. The Post Office was always having trouble holding its employees, as it had a top figure of $83.33 per month for clerks. The result was that as soon as a clerk found a job at the prevailing wage, he left the Post Office on short notice. My brother accepted a job there shortly after our arrival in Tonopah, but a day later was asked to work for the Nevada-California Power Co. as a lineman at six dollars per day. He had previously filed an application with this power company which supplied electric power to Tonopah and other Nevada camps from its generating plant on Bishop Creek, Inyo County, California. Naturally, he did not continue working at the Post Office.

Joe Nelson handled freight at the Tonopah station of the Tonopah & Goldfield Railroad. John Peters was a free lance, doing various jobs with the team and wagon he had acquired. Jack Roach was clerk in a law office.

I worked in the real estate and mining office of Edwards & Barlow, a firm active in various mining ventures, which also served as an agency for townsite lots in several camps and for business and residential properties in Tonopah. Our office was in the Brokers Exchange Building, a two story stone structure on Brougher Avenue, which belonged to Ben Edwards, Billy Douglas, Jim McQuillan and Frank Golden, owner of Reno's Hotel Golden.

Early in 1906 our bachelor group was increased by the addition of two more men. Lewis Robbins from England found a position with the Warren Richardson engineering office. Jim Tucker from Boston, a small man who was promptly dubbed the "Shrimp", went to work for the Post Office.

We now had an assorted group with California, Boston, New York, Philadelphia, Washington, D. C., and England represented. Needing more space, we decided to buy a lot on the hill toward Mount Butler near the location of the new school building. Here we built a board-and-batten house of fair size with bunks to take care of our gang. Behind it we put a tent-house, canvas over a frame, with wooden floor and sides. This was our kitchen and washroom. We arranged for a married couple to cook our dinners.

Domestic water was a serious problem in Tonopah, as in nearly all the camps. In many places it had to be hauled long distances by teams which themselves would use about half the water on a round trip. This was very costly. Tonopah had water service in the main part of town, piped 14 miles from Rye Patch, but the outlying sections were served only by tank and team. In our own case, we had water delivered at the rate of a dollar for 25 gallons, hauled four miles from springs north of town. With water this precious it had to be conserved, so after washing himself, one found other uses for it, such as washing potatoes and cleaning the house.

To bathe we stood in a washtub and sponged off with water heated on the stove. For more luxury we could patronize one of the barber shops, where for two dollars one had the privilege of waiting one's turn for a bath in a real tub. The ultimate in bathing luxury, of a sort, was advertised in the Tonopah *Daily Sun* for September 18, 1906: "Sponge Baths, Alcohol

Massage. Lady Attendant. Center Street, third door below Capitol Hotel."

The water situation gave John Peters the idea of going into the water delivery business. He rigged up an axle with two wheels and shafts on which he mounted a large sixty-gallon cask. It was amusing to see him on his rounds, sitting on top of the cask on the one-horse rig, delivering the water.

v. Health problems

Our new establishment worked out very well until one morning when Nelson woke up all broken out with red spots. Jokingly someone said he must have smallpox. After deliberation, we called a doctor and our informal diagnosis proved unfortunately correct. Dr. Hammond said he would have to notify Dr. Cunningham the health officer, and that we would be quarantined. We decided to get a nurse for Nelson, but that the rest of us would leave for parts unknown as soon as possible to avoid the quarantine, which was promptly placed. My brother and I had jobs we could not give up, but the others felt free to go out of town on a prospecting trip in the hills, using the Peters team and wagon.

The health officer was upset when he could find only two of us to vaccinate, although Gus and I had been vaccinated before we left New York. At all events, there were no other cases of smallpox in our group, although there was quite a lot of it in Tonopah at the time.

Nelson got along all right. Nurses were hard to find, but we finally engaged an elderly Irishman, a section hand on the railroad, to take care of him for six dollars a day. Dr. Hammond attended Nelson during his illness.

After his recovery the others returned and things went along on an even keel until Tucker, the "Shrimp", came down with diphtheria. This meant another quarantine for us unless we got out fast, which we did. We arranged for a nurse for Tucker and Dr. Clarke who attended him advised us all to take a shot of antitoxin. Of the five of us who then lived in the cabin, none was anxious to have a shot, but we were prevailed upon to do so.

Tucker had a bad time of it but finally pulled through and we moved back into our castle. During our enforced absence we rented rooms and had our meals in restaurants. It was not long after Tucker's illness that Robbins came down with pneumonia. This time it was necessary to move him to the Miners' Union Hospital in town, where he stayed for some time, as he was seriously ill.

At an elevation of over 6000 feet, Tonopah had a rigorous climate with hot summers and severe winters, cold and dry, with sometimes heavy snow. Pneumonia was of epidemic proportions, especially among the heavy drinkers, many of whom died within a couple of days after wandering out of hot saloons and gambling places with their clothes unbuttoned, exposing themselves to the chilling air.

vi. Social life

Our bachelor group was not unique in Tonopah. There were quite a few young single women who had positions as stenographers and clerks. In one instance six of them joined together as a spinster club, renting a large house for $100 a month. They were from various parts of the country and took an active part in the social affairs of the town.

Socially, Tonopah was a lively place, as it was in mining and business. There were parties galore in the homes of the elite and there was the Fortnightly Club. This was attended by ladies in the latest of evening attire, with escorts in tuxedos or dinner jackets. Sometimes a member, too deeply in his cups, might wander into the club wearing his working clothes, complete with high top boots, which were frowned upon in this setting.

When the Tonopah Mining Co. completed its mill at Miller's siding, 13 miles north of Tonopah on the railroad, the boys employed at the mill decided to give a dance and invited a group of us to join them. Ten of us brought our girls on the regular train to Miller's and had an enjoyable time at the dance until it broke up.

We thought that the Miller's crowd had arranged for our transportation back to Tonopah, but this turned out to be a misunderstanding. We were stranded and would have to do some explaining if we did not get the girls back home at a reasonable hour.

Automobiles were out of the question, as there were none in the area except for a couple on the Manhattan stage run. The only solution was the railroad. After considerable telephoning to Tonopah, we finally arranged with the railroad company to send a locomotive and a passenger car to Miller's to pick us up for the return to Tonopah. It cost us fifty dollars for the crowd and we were thankful to get off that easily.

vii.   Tonopah business

During the height of Tonopah's boom, three papers were published there, the weekly Tonopah *Miner* and two dailies, the *Sun* and the *Bonanza*. The *Sun* sold at a dime for a single sheet folded in half to make four pages. A San Francisco paper, which sold for five cents with many pages, once commented on the high price of the Tonopah papers. The *Sun* responded tartly that Tonopah people were liberal, not penurious, in their living.

There was an active Board of Trade and three banks in town, the Tonopah Banking Corporation, the State Bank & Trust Co. and the Nye & Ormsby County Bank. Among their officers and directors were such prominent Nevada names as Nixon, Brougher, Wingfield, Knox, Oddie, Mapes, Golden, and Alonzo Tripp.

Prominent attorneys included Key Pittman; Dennis & Warren, Campbell, Matson & Brown; Raymond D. Frisbie; McIntosh & Cooke and William Forman. Among the physicians and surgeons were Drs. J. R. Cunningham, E. K. Smith, H. V. King, Hammond and Clarke.

Prominent stores included the Tonopah Mercantile Co., Lothrop-Davis Co., John Gregovich, Jerry Ahern, and others.

viii.   Sports in Nevada

Ten of us formed the West End Tennis Club. We obtained permission from the West End Mining Co. to build a court on part of their property in the center of town. We prepared a dirt court, heavily rolled and packed, with a wire fence and a small adobe cabin to use as a change room and shower. To finance the court we charged a fifty dollar initiation fee.

While the tennis club, like the social clubs, was considered a bit highbrow at first, it soon took hold and provided plenty of entertainment. There were quite a few excellent players in town and we held regular tournaments. With the success of our court, two more were built on the Tonopah or Belmont Mining Co. property.

The Tonopah *Daily Sun* of Wednesday, July 18, 1906 said: "The Tonopah Tennis Club is going to make next Friday a gala day for sport in the opening of their new courts. A series of match doubles and singles will furnish sport for the afternoon. The team will be drawn from Messrs. Gore, Rounsevell, Hunter, Swan, Herbs, King and Billeb and others of equal ability." Many fine women players, too, added to the competition.

Nevada's biggest sporting event of the time was at Goldfield on Labor Day, 1906. For the largest purse yet posted in the prize ring, Joe Gans, considered the most scientific fighter of the day, met Battling Nelson, the tough lightweight challenger. The promoter was Tex Rickard, proprietor of Goldfield's Northern Saloon. An arena was built to accommodate 10,000 spectators at prices ranging from $5 to $25 per seat. After 42 rounds of slugging, Joe Gans was declared winner on a foul blow by Nelson. Nevada was the only state that would permit a fight to the finish.

After the successful promotion of this fight in Goldfield, people in Tonopah decided to put on their own match, not to be outdone by the rival camp. The promoters signed up the champion, Joe Gans, to fight Kid Herman. With no suitable arena in Tonopah, it was necessary to build one, no little task considering that lumber for the structure had to come a long way. Because of delays, much of the lumber had to be shipped by carload express at high prices. In many cases, for lack of proper sized beams, trusses had to be made by bolting two-inch lumber together. The fight was held as scheduled, but the arena was far from full. Gans won the fight in the eighth round, as I recall, though it looked as if he could have disposed of Herman at any time from the first round on.

ix.   Tonopah amusements

The Butler Theater in Tonopah had vaudeville shows and at one time Will King and his company from San Francisco's Casino Theater played there for a long engagement. In the Opera House was a roller skating rink, well attended by the younger crowd and by older people too.

As in all mining camps, Tonopah had a large red-light district. Its center was the Casino dance hall at the lower end of Main Street. The early days of the 49ers were reproduced here in rough and ready style. The hall had a large dance floor with a bar along one side and a balcony with partitioned sections overlooking the dance floor. The cost of a dance was fifty cents. The girls got a percentage of this and also of what their partners spent for drinks—and the more, the merrier.

The favorite tunes were "Turkey in the Straw" and "The Old Gray Mare." Dances were brief and the bigger the crowd the shorter the dance, with the spieler calling out his "hot" tunes as quickly as possible. A dancer was lucky if a tune lasted long enough to get around one side of the floor before another dance would be called.

A young, well-to-do Bostonian, in town to get acquainted with the mining districts and look for promising investments, decided to go to the Casino to see what it was like. When he got there the place was crowded and really rocking. Soon he remarked, "Let's get out of here. I promised my wife that I would not go anywhere I could not take her and I'm afraid this place would be out of the question."

Gambling was wide open of course, the saloons operating 24 hours a day. Fortunes were at stake on many occasions and there were no slot machines to distract from the main games of chance. A couple of saloons were a bit more refined in their clientele; one such place was Ritch's saloon at the back on the ground floor of the Brokers Exchange Building. Mining men gathered there in the late afternoon for heavy gambling. To liven things up a game would be started by throwing gold coins, of denominations agreed upon, to a line marked on the floor. The man whose coin landed nearest the line was the winner and took all. As quite a few would take part in the game, this was a way to win a good sum with quick action.

Many of the restaurants sold meal tickets, a five dollar ticket generally being good for six dollars worth of meals. It was not uncommon to have an acquaintance ask for your meal ticket to get a meal after an unfortunate night at the gambling tables. The favor was always reciprocated when fortune smiled on a prior loser.

The Tonopah Club was the largest and busiest saloon in town, but the many other places did their share of business too. One night I had just entered the long narrow saloon of the Tonopah Liquor Co. when a man entered behind me and started a commotion. He was in his cups and as the bouncer came up to take care of him, the man pulled a gun and aimed it at the bouncer, who made a grab for the gun just as the trigger was pulled, catching the web of skin and flesh of his right thumb and forefinger between the trigger and firing pin. At the same time the bouncer hit the drunk with his left hand, causing him to let go of the gun which then hung on the bouncer's right hand without discharging. This was about as close as one can get without being shot.

Talent for Tonopah's night spots had to be versatile. An advertisement in the *Daily Sun* said, "Wanted—a piano player; must be a good dishwasher. Apply Glad Hand Bar."

x. *The mining business*

In my work at the Edwards & Barlow office I became familiar with some of the intricacies of the mining business as it was practiced in Nevada in those days. I also learned something of the history of the town.

Tonopah—named with the Indian word for "water brush"— is in the extreme western portion of Nevada's Nye County, near the Esmeralda County line. It is located in a dry desert country at about the 6000 foot elevation, at the foot of taller mountains. The nearest water is about four miles to the northeast.

Jim Butler, discoverer of Tonopah, made his original discovery on a prospecting trip between Belmont, then the county seat, and the southern Klondyke Mining District. While accounts vary as to how he made the discovery, the most accepted one is as follows:

The evening of May 18, 1900, he camped at the spring northeast of the mountain then known as Sawtooth Peak. The following morning he went out to round up his burros that had strayed up the side of the peak from his camp. He noticed some outcroppings of a ledge and took samples that looked promising. He continued on to the southern Klondyke district and returned later to Belmont, taking the ore samples along with him.

Several months later the samples were assayed by C. Cayhart in Austin, through the efforts of Tasker L. Oddie, a friend of the Butlers, who later became governor and United States Senator from Nevada. The assays from the samples showed values up to $300 per ton of ore, enough to cause Butler and Oddie to return to the place of Butler's discovery. Mining claims were located on August 27, 1900, before the discovery was generally known to the public. The original group owning the first claims were Butler and his wife, Oddie, Cayhart and Wilse Brougher, a friend of the Butlers and Sheriff of Nye County.

Once the news of the discovery became generally known, the rush was on. Leases were let to friends of the original locators and others, many making fortunes before selling the properties. In 1902 Butler sold his original property, including the famous Mizpah mine, to the Tonopah Mining Co., an eastern investors' syndicate.

The original prospectors left their marks in the names of the peaks in the area. Sawtooth Peak was renamed Mount Oddie and two other peaks on the west side of the town were named Mount Brougher and Mount Butler.

In 1904 the three-foot gauge Tonopah Railroad was built, connecting with the Carson & Colorado near Sodaville, about sixty miles north of Tonopah. It is reported that the cost of construction of this line was repaid within six months from the heavy traffic and high rates. It was soon widened to standard gauge and, in connection with the extension of the railroad in Goldfield in 1905, provided through service to the newer camp at Goldfield that threatened to surpass even Tonopah in production.

At the time of my arrival in Tonopah, standard gauging had recently been completed. The Goldfield extension had been in operation for a month and within another month the two railroads were to be combined as the Tonopah & Goldfield Railroad.

Shortly after my arrival, mills and cyanide plants were built for the treatment of ores, the largest of these being that of the Tonopah Mining Co. at Millers, 13 miles to the northwest.

Tonopah's population reached its peak of about 14,000 around 1908. The United States Geological Survey estimates the mineral production of the Tonopah district from 1900 to 1920 to have aggregated about 120 million dollars, with silver predominating.

Tonopah was booming along in high gear when I arrived, as were Goldfield and other camps with new discoveries of gold and silver, such as Bullfrog, Rhyolite, Manhattan, and Wonder.

xi. Investments

The mining men who came to the Edwards & Barlow office, where I worked, invested heavily in the Tonopah mines and also in the new discoveries. New companies were formed to raise funds for development. Restrictions on forming these companies were not severe and it was usual for the incorporators to secure promising mining locations for development by cash purchase, plus stock in the new corporation, thus forming a million share company with a par value of a dollar per share.

Generally six or seven hundred thousand shares would be issued to the original owners of the claims and to the parties who were promoting them. This stock would be pooled and held in escrow so that it could not be sold to the general public for a specified time. The balance of the stock, three to four hundred thousand shares, would be set aside as treasury stock to be offered to the public for whatever it might bring, say from ten cents to a dollar per share, depending on the attractiveness of the mining property.

Incorporation was generally under the laws of South Dakota, where for a fee of $53 you could charter a million share corporation and be in business. Many of these corporations, of course, fell by the wayside. Sometimes they were unable to raise enough capital, through sale of treasury stock, to develop the property. Other times the mining property did not produce as much ore as had been expected. Usually the incorporators were the only losers.

I was once asked to incorporate a company to take over a group of mining claims in the Wonder Mining District in Churchill County, about 55 miles east of Fallon. This district, at an elevation of 5800 feet was newly discovered in 1906. The company was called the Bumble Bee Wonder Mining Co. Circulars, advertisements and other promotional materials were sent to prospective buyers of the stock, from a long list of stockholders in other mining companies. Unfortunately it was not a good time for the promotion, and it failed. I was the only one who was "stung", having advanced the funds for stationery, stamps, and so on, for which I was not reimbursed. Despite the failure of this particular promotion, the Wonder District produced about six million dollars in gold, silver, copper and zinc during the ensuing fifteen years, mostly from the Nevada Wonder mine.

Whenever a new strike was reported, there was all sorts of speculation. Soon a new townsite would be laid out and lots put up for sale. Sometimes there would be a rush for lots to establish a business or to gamble on an increase in price if the camp should develop. If it did not, you were out your money.

At times, there were certain requirements to be met by the purchaser of a lot. During the Greenwater boom, for instance, a purchaser was required to spend at least a thousand dollars for a building. Since the cost of timber hauled in for long distance by teams was very high, that money would be hardly enough for a shed. Greenwater, in the Black Mountains near the southeastern boundary of Death Valley National Monument, did not last long.

xii.   Nearby mining districts

About thirty miles southwest of Tonopah, in Esmeralda County, was another mining prospect that showed good promise. The Silver Peak District had been discovered in 1864 and was a small producer up to 1900, when its output sharply increased. In 1906 the Silver Peak Railroad was completed from Blair Junction, on the Tonopah & Goldfield, to Silver Peak, a town about twenty miles away. At this time a large mill was also constructed at Blair, near Silver Peak.

We were interested in the Valcalda Junior Mining Co., adjoining the Valcalda mine, located on the hill some distance from Silver Peak. With a man named Beauchamp, I drove over from Tonopah and camped on the property for several days to do some work on the mining claims.

While there we heard about a new find at Cottonwood, about ten or twelve miles away. The discovery was by Harry Stimler, the discoverer of the "Grandpa" or Goldfield District. We drove over to Cottonwood and found a group of prospectors and mining people already on the ground. It seemed as though everyone who had a mining claim located within miles of the place was looking for a buyer on whom to unload. We soon went back to our own diggings. Cottonwood's boom was short-lived.

One of the companies that we organized, the New Klondyke Mining Co. gave considerable promise. The mine was about 15 miles to the south of Tonopah in the Klondyke Mining District, Esmeralda County. Jim Butler had been headed for this district on a prospecting trip when he discovered the ore at Tonopah. We raised money for the purchase and development through the sale of stock. Several shipments of ore went to the smelters before the vein pinched out and further development had to be stopped for lack of funds. Among the big expenses in this operation was the need for hauling water all the way from Tonopah.

The Manhattan District was discovered in 1905. It is located at an elevation of about 6900 feet in Nye County, about fifty miles north of Tonopah. When word of the discovery of rich ore there reached Tonopah the rush was on. One Sunday morning three of us climbed to the summit of Mount Butler, where we watched the procession of teams, mules, burros, people afoot and on horseback, stages, wagons and all kinds of conveyances streaming toward the new discovery.

Merchants and other businessmen rushed to the new camp to cash in on it. Tents were set up for stores, bars and other accommodations. One merchant put up a large tent with cots for sleeping. Here one could rent a cot for eight hours, when someone else would crawl into it. A canvas partition stretched across the back of the tent to separate the men's from the women's section.

During the latter part of 1907 I went to Manhattan to do some assessment work on the mining claims of the Manhattan Marvel Mining Co. which we had incorporated the previous year. I took a contract and had my first experience in actual mining work.

I will always remember the first time I had to handle the dynamite and caps used for blasting. I carried the dynamite under my coat as it was bitter cold and I had some distance to go on foot to the claims. Needless to say, I was damned nervous.

During the time I was with Edwards & Barlow, the firm was concerned with the organization of other companies, including the Gilt Edge Mining Co., with claims in the Transvaal District in southern Nye County, and also the Goldyke Mining Co., in the district of the same name, discovered by Workman and Davis, two well known prospectors. Goldyke is about 35 miles northeast of Luning, a station on the Southern Pacific.

A couple of my friends joined me in locating some mining claims near Gold Mountain, later better known as the Divide District, six miles south of Tonopah on the road to Goldfield. Nothing came of our venture, but after 1912 the district became an important producer of gold and silver.

While Tonopah was a big center for silver, Goldfield mines were mostly gold. Goldfield was first discovered by Harry Stimler and William Marsh in December 1902, but the rush to the new camp did not take place until about a year later with the discovery of high grade ore. The Tonopah & Goldfield Railroad reached Goldfield in 1905 and numerous mills were built. In 1908 Goldfield had a population of 20,000. Its production from 1903 to 1921 is reported as almost 85 million dollars.

xiii. Labor troubles and business slump

There was considerable labor trouble in Tonopah and Goldfield around 1906 and 1907 with the Industrial Workers of the World trying to organize the miners and other groups. Mining companies and other business people opposed this. Things became hectic at times and once quite a few of the I.W.W. group were rounded up in Goldfield and locked up in a boxcar of the Tonopah & Goldfield. When the train arrived in Tonopah a committee met it and refused to let the occupants out of the car. The train took them along to Hazen, I believe, before they were released.

The San Francisco earthquake and fire of April, 1906, had a depressing effect on the mining section, especially Manhattan, where a great deal of San Francisco capital had been invested. Operations slowed down and it was some time until activity resumed at full scale.

During the latter part of 1907 the mining camps quieted down from the boom of 1901-1906. The financial panic of that year was felt even in Nevada. Matters were not helped by the failure of the State Bank & Trust Co. and the Nye & Ormsby County Bank in Tonopah.

Businesses curtailed operations or failed. Employees were laid off. Presently, like many another young man in Nevada who had chosen employment more lucrative than that offered by the Post Office, I found myself without a job, along with several of the others in our bachelor group.

xiv. Cutting cordwood

It was necessary for those of us who were out of work to get busy. Peters and I decided to go out in the hills to cut cordwood and ship it to town. There was a serious shortage of coal and wood for use in the homes and prices were very high. Cordwood four feet long was bringing from $30 to $35 per cord.

Peters had a light wagon and had broken a team of cayuses to drive. We loaded up with our supplies, bedding, tent and other camping equipment and headed for piñon pine country about forty miles northeast of Tonopah. We left at about noon October 22, 1907, and arrived at Kinney stage station late that night and set up camp. Because of the load we walked about seven miles.

The next evening we reached the camp of a cowpuncher we knew, a man named Wilson, and stayed over for a day. Then we moved on, along a "road" that was nothing but a pair of ruts through the sand and sagebrush, off the beaten path and untraveled except for an occasional wood team. We walked the last five miles through the rain until we reached the camp of old man Hartle.

Hartle lived the life of a hermit in a one-room cabin, built of rock and mud, with a fireplace where he cooked his meals. The rain leaked through the thatched roof onto the dirt floor, making it a sloppy place. It was the worst place we had ever seen, but we took advantage of his hospitality to the extent of cooking our meal in the fireplace. We chose to sleep under our wagon. I will never forget how wet and frosty it was in the morning. After a sorry attempt at breakfast and feeding the horses, we left for the timber where we expected to establish a camp.

By the time we arrived at the planned campsite, it was dark. Though we had been told that there was water nearby we could find none. We had brought enough water for our personal use but none for the horses. As it was late for us to hunt for a possible spring, Peters led the horses up a canyon that showed signs of water at its upper end. I stayed in camp to prepare supper.

It was several hours before he returned with the horses. He had found some water but too far from our camp. The following day we dug a well in a gulch half a mile from our camp. About eight feet below the surface we found water that served our needs, after the silt settled. We had to pack it on the horses in five-gallon cans we had brought for the purpose.

Cutting the wood was a tough job for us and we worked at it several days before we were hardened to the toil. We kept at the cutting until we had a load of ten cords ready for the teamster who was to haul the wood to Tonopah for us, according to arrangements made prior to our leaving town. He and his team were to be at our camp in ten days with supplies for us and hay and grain for the horses.

While we were there cutting wood, the nights grew very cold and for several days it snowed. Fortunately we had plenty of bedding and spent most of the time sleeping in the tent. Our cook stove was in the open a short distance from the front of the tent. Twice during nights we found that the front end of our tent had collapsed and we found sections of the tent ropes missing. In cleaning frying pans and pots we had carelessly thrown grease and garbage so that it covered the ropes; coyotes had slipped in nights and chewed up the delicious tent ropes, causing our tent to fall in.

The wood team, twelve horses and two wagons, arrived about four days late. During the last couple of days we had to eat jackrabbits Peters shot. We loaded the wagons and started for Tonopah but made only three miles from camp. With no road, it was hard pulling for the team.

That night Peters and I had to return to our well for a supply of water for ourselves and our teams. The teamster had a couple of barrels on his wagon, each of about thirty gallons capacity. We also took along our five gallon cans. It was pitch dark when we arrived at the well. We filled the barrels and cans and started on the return trip. The wagon we were using had sides ten inches high and I tried to steady the barrels while Peters drove. It was hard going in the gulch and the wagon hit a boulder a short distance from the well. The sharp lurch caused me to be thrown off the wagon with one of the barrels of water. Fortunately the barrel landed on the ground and not on me, but it was smashed and I received a good soaking. We finally managed to return to camp with the rest of the water intact.

The following day we made it to Antelope Springs, a distance of eight miles. From that point there was some semblance of a road. There was nothing at the so-called spring except a water hole used by stock and animals roaming the hills. By the next night we had reached Rye Patch, some ten miles. From there to Tonopah was a good road and we arrived in town the following night. The forty miles had taken us just four days.

The teamster's charge for hauling the wood was $10 per cord and an additional $1.50 per cord stumpage went to the Forest Service. We had no trouble disposing of the wood at $30 per cord.

After a few days resting in Tonopah, we started again for our wood camp, this time with my brother Gus joining the party. We made arrangements with another teamster to haul our next ten cords at $8 per cord. The team was to come for the load in a week, but it did not show up. We waited several days longer until our food ran very low. Finally we started back to Tonopah, this time making it in two days. The teamster had left for other places and with stormy weather in prospect, we could find no one else to haul the wood for us, so our labor was in vain. This ended the wood business for us.

xv. Bleak Christmas

Christmas was now approaching and the prospect of the holiday looked bleak for our bachelor group, most of us out of work and our funds almost exhausted. Fortunately my brother Gus and I had ten dollars, a gift from our sisters in New York. After a conference with the boys, it was decided that the ten dollars were hardly enough to provide a big feed and refreshments worthy of the season. So Gus took the money and we accompanied him to the Tonopah Club to see what he could do to replenish our cash reserves in his favorite game, faro. His luck ebbed and flowed—and with it, our spirits—but he finally accumulated fifty dollars. At this point we prevailed on him to quit. At last we were able to have a merry Christmas.

Some of our group moved away and finally there remained in our bachelor quarters only four of us who had been fortunate in finding employment again after a brief lapse. Robbins had a position with Warren Richardson whose office did a good part of the surveying and engineering work for the mining companies. Peters did miscellaneous work around town with his team. Gus worked in a grocery store. Once more I was with Edwards & Barlow and part of the time with the West End Mining Co.

xvi.   Surveying in a mine

During an idle period one of Richardson's engineers asked if I would help him with some underground work surveying the Tonopah Midway mine. The purpose of this work was to measure distances and directions of drifts, crosscuts, winzes, raises and so on, along the veins of ore and otherwise. After obtaining this information in the survey, we would then plot it on maps of the mine.

I agreed to go along as chainman for surveyor Ed Dodge. At the Midway hoisting works we boarded a cage for the trip down the shaft and worked on several levels. At the 200-foot level there was a short drift which had never been surveyed or mapped. Here we unloaded our instruments and went to work.

Dodge set up his transit and sighted along the drift as we made the measurement to the face. The drift had been run on both sides of the shaft and Dodge found he could sight the face of the drift in the opposite direction across the shaft without resetting the transit. Now I had to measure the distance with the tape.

As I recall, the Midway shaft was 800 feet deep at the time. It was a three-compartment shaft, with cages in two of the compartments. The third was a manway, cluttered with ladders, pump column, air pipes and other equipment. To measure the distance Dodge wanted, I had to cross the shaft to the other side. At the time, both cages were in operation, hoisting ore or waste from the lower levels of the mine, and running at high speed.

After one of the cages passed our level on its way to the surface, I jumped across the shaft, not wanting to work my way through the manway. The measurement made, I prepared to jump back across the shaft. There had been some delay in the hoisting and I looked up the shaft to see if the cage in that compartment was at the surface. There was light showing under the cage to indicate that it was at the surface. I jumped across. To my amazement and shock, I barely missed being hit by the cage on its downward trip and the seat of my pants felt as though they had been scorched. I landed safely on the floor of the drift and Dodge almost collapsed from fright at my narrow escape. After we recovered our composure we decided to call it a day.

xvii. Drifting away

As in all mining camps when the "bloom of the boom" has subsided, people not in business or steadily employed at Tonopah gradually drifted away to other places that appeared more promising, or perhaps returned, somewhat disappointed, to the old home towns. Tonopah settled down to a more conservative basis. People built better housing for themselves than had been available during the hectic days of the boom. The most successful people began to put up fine large residences.

Our bachelor group gradually broke up as we went our various ways. My brother continued with the grocery firm where he was employed. In my case, an opportunity presented itself that made me face the decision whether to remain in thriving Tonopah or to move more than 100 miles west to an old camp that had seen better days, Bodie, Mono County, California.

Reno was a solid city when I first came there in 1905. The view above is across the Southern Pacific tracks to the southeast toward the corner of Commercial Row and Virginia Street. I spent the night in the Overland Hotel, just off the picture to the left. The stagecoach below is about to leave Tonopah for Sodaville and Mina. The sign on the roof of the building reads, "Lothrop & Davis, General Merchandise." By the time I reached Tonopah, that store was in a larger building uptown.

I stayed at the Merchants Hotel my first night in Tonopah. Below is a jerk-line team at the head of two heavy loads of lumber, with a feed wagon at the rear.

Even on a donkey, during those days in Tonopah, I sometimes wore fine clothes and a watch chain. On the ground floor of the building in the middle picture on this page was the Post Office. Dr. Hammond's office was upstairs. At the right is our board-and-batten bachelor residence with its tent-house kitchen in the rear.

Tonopah's Main Street, below, leads south toward the headframe of the Jim Butler mine and Mount Butler. The Mizpah Hotel and the tall building of the State Bank & Trust Co., across the street, were new when I was there. At the bottom of the opposite page is a group of Tonopah's elite. Ella Cain, my future sister-in-law, is at the upper left of the group.

The West End Tennis Club used a court on West End Mining Co. property. The Nye County Court House, below, was newly finished when I came to Tonopah. The pictures on the other page date from about 1902 and show how tiny Tonopah was three years before I came. The upper view is south along Main Street toward Mount Butler; the other is of Mount Brougher, looking across Main Street from the east. The Mizpah shaft is in the foreground.

The panorama is over Tonopah toward the east, from the side of Mount Brougher. The dark patch at the foot of Mount Oddie is the hoisting works of the Tonopah Mining Co. The always enthusiastic Fourth of July celebration is shown in the lower pictures. In the double-jack drilling

TONOPAH NEV. 1905.

E.W. SMITH
PHOTO.

contest, left, one man wields the heavy hammer while his partner holds
the octagonal shaft of the drill, giving it a partial turn between blows.
Front and center in the big parade at the right is one of Tonopah's few
automobiles, gaily decorated and paced by the inevitable dog.

I drove that two-horse team about 15 miles south of Tonopah to deliver the payroll to the New Klondyke mine, where the above photograph was taken. The lower picture dates from about 1903, perhaps while Goldfield was still known as the Grandpa Mining District. Mining was then booming and feverish building activity soon changed the appearance of the place greatly.

MAIN ST.
GOLDFIELD NEV.

These stock certificates both represented mining properties in the Bull-frog Mining District, near Beatty and Rhyolite, Nevada. My holdings in these companies didn't earn me anything, but I didn't lose either, and the certificates are nice souvenirs. They would make good wallpaper.

This picture, looking east over Bodie, was made about 1910. The snowshed from the Bulwer tunnel to the Standard mill is that dark horizontal line from the left of the picture. In the foreground is Bodie's cemetery with the mortuary just beyond, to the right. High on the ridge above it can be seen the railroad office on the hill.

CHAPTER TWO

NEW JOB ON THE BODIE RAILROAD

i. Lumber for the mines

In contrast to big, new, bustling Tonopah, the boom town of the early 1900s, Bodie was a mining camp in Mono County, California that dated from the 1860s with a colorful reputation for rich ore strikes and bad men. Its boom years came around 1880 when some ten thousand people swarmed its treeless sagebrush flat at an elevation of 8375 feet, a score of miles east of the county seat at Bridgeport and half a dozen miles west of the Nevada state line.

Remote as it was, the camp's feverish mining activity of the boom years brought a pressing need for lumber, poles and cordwood. The wagons that hauled in lumber for sawmills in the Bridgeport and Mono Lake areas could not keep up with the demand for construction timber. Chinamen packing in cordwood on burros were hard pressed to keep the mining machinery going and, during severe winter cold to keep the insides of the buildings warm.

Timber grew in the mountains some thirty miles to the south, on the other side of Mono Basin. A railroad would make this supply more readily available to the mines. In 1881 the Bodie Railway & Lumber Co. was organized. It constructed a three-foot-gauge line 32 miles to Mono Saw Mills in the mountains to the south of Mono Lake. Here were set up railroad shops, lumber mills, logging camps and all that was necessary to serve as the center of a large lumbering and cordwood operation. By December that year the railroad was in operation.

Initial operations were so successful that the company decided to extend a branch line from Warm Springs station on the east side of Mono Lake to Benton, California, where it was to meet the narrow gauge Carson & Colorado, then being built by D. Ogden Mills. This would connect the now-isolated Bodie line with the outside world and would make it possible to ship lumber from Mono Mills to points south along the C. & C., which was planned to go all the way to the Colorado River.

The name of the company, accordingly, was changed in 1882 to the Bodie & Benton Railway & Commercial Co. A line was surveyed from Warm Springs to Benton and nine miles had been graded when suddenly work ceased. No explanation was even given the public, but it was assumed that the Mills interests looked with disfavor on the competition this would bring to lumber mills they controlled in the Lake Tahoe area, since Mono Mills lumber shipped over the proposed connection could have undersold the Tahoe product that had to be hauled all the way down from Carson City on the Carson & Colorado Railroad.

The Bodie & Benton never reached Benton and always remained isolated. Its fortunes rose and fell with the prosperity of the mines in the vicinity of Bodie. When the new gold rush developed in the Tonopah and Goldfield regions in the early 1900s, new possibilities for the Bodie & Benton came into prospect.

In 1906 the property of the Bodie & Benton Railway & Commercial Co. was taken over by a syndicate headed by Charles E. Knox, president of the Montana-Tonopah Mining Co., with Mark B. Kerr, consulting engineer of West End Mining Co., as chief engineer. They organized the Mono Lake Railway & Lumber Co. and their purpose was to build a broad gauge line from Mono Mills and easterly from Mono Lake to connect with the Tonopah & Goldfield at Sodaville. Thus, in addition to supplying wood and timber to Bodie, Aurora and nearby camps, they would be able to supply lumber, poles, wood, lime and supplies to the mines of Tonopah, Goldfield and other camps in southern Nevada.

In 1908 the company was incorporated as the Mono Lake Lumber Co. Mr. Kerr was appointed to superintend the operation. He asked me to move to Bodie and take a position on the railroad there. This seemed to offer the prospect of a responsible position, particularly if the broad gauge line were built, so I accepted Mr. Kerr's offer and arranged to move to Bodie.

I went with Mr. Kerr to Bodie in early April, 1908. We took the train from Tonopah to Thorne, thence by stage seven miles to Hawthorne, where we transferred to the six-horse Concord stage for the 35-mile trip across the state line to Bodie.

ii. Railroad office on the hill

Bodie turned out to be a large camp of weatherbeaten houses, inhabited by no more than 300 people, on a treeless plain at the foot of snow-covered hills. The streets were muddy from the melting snow which still stood in untidy piles about the town. Boardwalks lined either side of Main Street. All this was quite different from Tonopah with its substantial buildings and larger population.

My own circumstances were quite different from what they had been in 1905 when I arrived in Tonopah, unknown, needing a place to live and a job. Here at Bodie I came as a representative of the new management of the railway and lumber company and was first put up at the Occidental Hotel. Soon I moved to the railroad office building on the hill. This was a solid two-story structure, well built on a stone foundation, substantial enough to withstand the heavy storms and high winds that often buffeted the hilltop.

The main floor was mostly a large room used as the office. It had a counter running along two sides, with the usual high desks and stools behind it. There was a large safe with "Bodie Bank" lettered above the doors. Adjoining the main office was a smaller room with desk and office furniture; this was my private office.

Behind the main office was the kitchen and a room sometimes used for boarding train crews; further back was the woodshed and beyond that the toilet, under cover. Upstairs was a large room used as a sitting room or bedroom, and four smaller bedrooms.

Heat was provided by wood stoves. Coal oil and gasoline lamps were used for illumination until electricity became available, about 1912. Water had to be laboriously packed in buckets from the town reservoir on the hilltop, a couple of hundred yards away from the office building. This was a particularly difficult chore during winter storms and cold. At such times we melted snow on the stoves to furnish water for washing and cleaning.

The overflow pipe line from Rough Creek Springs, about five miles away, brought water to the reservoir, which also served in winter as a source for ice, harvested when eight or more inches thick. It was cut and stored under sawdust in ice houses and sheds to preserve it for summer use in Bodie's saloons, restaurants, hotels and stores.

Also on the hill was the Bodie terminal's big barn. Every morning and evening the horses had to be led nearly a quarter of a mile to the reservoir for water. It was a struggle to get them there in the winter, what with pushing a trail through the deep snow and breaking ice in the reservoir to get at the water.

In the railroad yard were several sidings where the cordwood, lumber and poles were unloaded from the cars and stacked. There was also a platform for loading supplies and other material on the cars for shipment to Mono Mills. Quite often a saddle horse or team would be loaded on a car that was prepared with a suitable enclosure for the animals. Sometimes automobiles which were to tour the country south of Mono Mills would avoid the long trip around Mono Lake by being loaded on the railroad cars.

iii. Violent dispute

The railroad's books were in bad shape and my first task on the new job was to put them in order. Because of incomplete records, there was much misunderstanding and bad feeling among some of the contractors who cut and hauled logs, wood, poles and timber to the logging camp at the end of the railroad, four miles south of Mono Mills. We spent several days going over books and records with the contractors but found that the claims and counterclaims would take some time to reconcile.

Mr. Kerr decided to return to Tonopah until an audit could be completed.

Meanwhile, the contractors were asking for payment of their accounts, claiming considerably more to their credit above advance payments, bills for supplies for their boardinghouse and feed bills for their stock, of which there were about thirty head of horses and mules. They had teamsters, helpers, loggers and others to pay, and no one had taken the trouble to strike a balance.

Our audit indicated that the amount due the contractors was much less than they claimed, much of the difference being accounted for by the bills charged at the bar in an old shack on the premises. We advised Mr. Kerr of the final figures and he returned to Bodie a few days later. We all went to Mono Mills to try to work out a satisfactory settlement with Young and Collins, the hauling contractors, and with John Yribarren, who had the contract for cutting logs, cordwood and poles.

We held our meeting in the corner of the commissary, where an office enclosure had been set off with a waist-high railing and gate. In this enclosure were a high desk and a safe that consisted of the front door of a vault, with the inner door making up the back and shelves built in between the two doors. Mr. Kerr, Ed Rapp, the clerk and I were inside the railing, the contractors outside.

We explained how their accounts stood and the balance due them according to our audit. This was considerably less than they expected and they promptly disputed our figures. The arguments between Young and Collins — who had apparently indulged a bit before the meeting — and Kerr got out of hand. When the dispute became heated, Young and Collins suddenly pulled out guns and hit Kerr on the side of the head, cutting his scalp and ear, and felling him to the floor.

Rapp was sitting on a stool at the desk and I was standing at the gate of the enclosure behind Kerr when he was hit. I then moved out, walked over and told Young and Collins that there was no reason for this. My action proved foolish, as a gun was pointed at my face and I was told that my head would be blown off. I backed away to the rear of the store, the gun following me closely until I could move no further. The barrel looked big enough to crawl into.

At that point the contractors decided to pull out and settle matters later. I wanted Kerr to go to Bridgeport with me to swear out a warrant for assault against Young and Collins, but this meant a 45-mile trip with a team, probably requiring two days. Kerr decided against it. Later the contractors moved out, taking their teams and employees. We sent a check to settle their account and the matter was ended as far as Young and Collins were concerned.

iv. "Case of the $1000 bandana"

In the case of John Yribarren, settlement took longer, for about 1500 cords of wood piled in the forest had to be measured, as well as a million feet of logs and 20,000 feet of poles scattered over a large area. He contested our figures and brought suit for a settlement based on his claims.

The case was settled out of court, between counsel, and had its humorous side. I like to call it the "case of the $1000 bandana handkerchief." It came about during the taking of depositions in the railroad office in the Bodie yards. Pat R. Parker, later judge of the Mono County Superior Court, represented Yribarren and Judge Campbell of San Francisco represented the lumber company.

Yribarren was questioned about various claims charged to him on the books of the company, such as supplies for his camp and employees. This included cash advances, for which no receipts signed by Yribarren could be found. He did not dispute these items, but claimed that he had cut more timber than had been credited to him.

Because he did not dispute the unverified items, the interrogation went smoothly until everything was spoiled by a bit of misplaced humor. We came to a separate item of $1.25 for a bandana handkerchief. He said he did not recall it. Jokingly, someone said, "Why, John, you probably bought it for one of those Indian squaws at Mono Mills."

Yribarren flushed and blew sky high as he denied that. A Spanish Basque, he had difficulty with English under normal circumstances. Now it was some time until he was calm enough to continue with the questioning. He refused to acknowledge any more charges unless we could produce a receipt. One of the items was an advance of $1000 cash, soon after the bandana handkerchief item. No amount of questioning could induce him to acknowledge this charge and it was not included in the final settlement.

The unfortunate attempt at humor about that bandana cost the company $1000. It was an expensive handkerchief!

v. Runaway team

At the time of this episode I had recently been appointed superintendent of the lumber company, in place of Perry Sexton, who was now staying at Hammond Station — now known as Tioga Lodge — on the west shore of Mono Lake. Our attorneys, trying to prove the charges disputed by Yribarren, wanted an affidavit from Sexton that the entries on the books were correct as listed. I was delegated to go to Hammond's for his affidavit.

I hired a team from the Cain stable in Bodie. As I climbed into the buggy, the stableman, Bob Sherman, warned me to be careful as one of the horses had a habit of switching his tail over the lines and if he caught one he would immediately try to run away. The team was spirited but I reached the bottom of the canyon without trouble.

When I approached the Scanavino Ranch, also known as the Goat Ranch, about ten miles from Bodie, I must have been a little careless. The horse caught one of the lines under his tail and away we went on a dead run. At places we left the road and bounced over the sagebrush. What with holding onto the rig to keep from flying out, and reaching over the dashboard to snap the line loose, it was some distance before I could get it released. At last I brought the team under control and continued on to Mono Lake.

At the John Mattly place, now Mono Inn, I stopped to pick up a notary by the name of Benedict. When Benedict came out, he stopped short and told me he would not get into any rig with that team of horses, as he knew they ran away at every opportunity. Needless to say, I did not tell him that this had already happened to me; I said to get in, as the team was O.K.

The road along the lake was then a narrow wagon road, lined on each side with willows and brush most of the way to Hammond's. As soon as Benedict was seated and we started out, the runaway started again with a wild ride over the rough road, but we managed to get the team under control before we reached Hammond's station.

We found Sexton in the old saloon with Hammond, Bill Rector and several others, all strangers to me at that time. They were all feeling pretty good and they told Sexton not to sign the affidavit. I convinced him that he would be in real trouble if he did not do so, as he would be liable for the monies charged to Yribarren. Finally he executed the affidavit before Benedict, the notary.

The return to Bodie was uneventful and I was careful not to let the team get out of control again. The horses were tired, too, as it was a twenty-mile trip each way. Forty miles in a day is a hard drive for a team of horses, with rough roads and heavy grades.

vi. Writ of attachment

Yribarren's attorney secured a writ of attachment on the logs and cordwood in the timber, pending settlement of his claims against the company. Meanwhile the company could not move nor use any of this attached wood in its operations. To serve the attachment papers on me as manager in charge of the lumber company, Sheriff Jim Dolan, a rangy six-footer, had to ride to Mono Mills from Bridgeport, a distance of 45 miles.

That morning, as it happened, I had left the Mills with several friends on horseback to do a little fishing at the Thompson Ranch, ten miles away. When Dolan did not find me at the

Mills on his arrival, he asked the sawmill foreman to accompany him and show him the road through the timber to the place where we were fishing. There were many roads, such as they were, used for hauling the logs and cordwood and anyone not acquainted with them could waste considerable time. Matt Thomas, the foreman, had no horse available, but he managed to borrow a burro from a sheepman who was camped at Mono Mills.

The sheriff and Matt started out and met our party several miles from our fishing spot. It was a sight to behold: the sheriff a tall thin man on an exceptionally large horse; beside him on a burro with only a blanket for a saddle sat the short, heavy foreman, his feet hanging down within a couple of inches from the ground. It was certainly the "long and short of it." We all had a good laugh and returned to the Mills for a libation.

Sheriff Dolan did his duty and served me with the attachment. Next morning he returned to Bridgeport and we had to be sure not to use any of the logs or cordwood covered by the attachment. Fortunately for us, we also had wood, cut by other contractors, which we could use for our operations.

vii. An old adversary

There was a sequel to the dispute of the contractors that occurred about three years later. Stuart Cain and I were on a trip from Bodie to Reno in a seven-passenger Thomas car. Our route was by way of Bodie Canyon, Sweetwater, and Wellington, where W. E. Reading, an old friend, had a general store. It was our habit to stop at Wellington to see if they wanted anything taken to Reno or for us to bring back for them.

This time dusk was gathering as we arrived at Wellington, and Stuart went into the store while I remained with the auto. He came out in a few minutes to say that nothing was wanted this time, but a man needed a ride to Carson City. It was urgent for him to get there as soon as possible and no other transportation was available until the next day's stage.

I told Stuart to bring him out, but he warned me that I ought to know that it was Collins, one of the contractors who had pulled a gun on us at Mono Mills. Now he was a deputy sheriff of Inyo County and was on the track of a horse thief reported heading for Carson. It seemed all right to me to take him along with us now.

Collins came out, climbed in the auto, and no word was spoken as we left for Carson City, hitting the road as fast as we could. We covered the bumpy 45 miles quickly, for those times, and finally stopped in front of the Arlington Hotel in Carson. Collins climbed out and came to the front of the car, asking if I remembered him. I said it was not likely that I would forget him. He apologized for the rumpus at Mono Mills and wanted to buy me a drink. We all went to have a couple of drinks and forget any hard feelings.

I never did hear if he caught the horse thief he was after.

viii. The railroad

The railroad had changed very little from the time it was built until I first saw it in 1908. The impressions of a Bodie journalist of the early days were so much like my own, and so graphically set forth in the *Weekly Standard-News* for August 10 and October 12, 1881, and January 11, 1882, that I cannot improve upon them:

[At Bodie station] vast quantities of lumber and wood are piled up along the track of the road, teams are constantly hauling up to the Standard shaft and other points, engines are running about here and there, presenting altogether a scene of great activity, differing essentially from the listlessness which is now-a-days the normal condition of Main Street . . .

A telegraph line has been run the entire length of the road to which telephones have been attached and by means of which communication is had between the various stations.

The train started about half past nine a.m. and was soon winding about among the hills on its way to the valley below. The constant changes of scene and variety of views render this part of the route quite picturesque. The grade is very steep, being . . . notwithstanding the many turns that are made around the hills . . . two hundred feet to the mile . . [About six and one half miles from Bodie] is the first switchback and about a mile and a half further is the second and only other one on the road. Between these two points . . . trains have to be backed both going down and coming up. Two miles beyond by the railroad route, and only three quarters of a mile direct, there was a great deal of heavy work done. Deep cuts had to be made in many places . . . and considerable filling had to be done . . . A trestle work was built 260 feet in length and 50 feet deep . . .

Mono Lake soon came in view with its solitary islands and its mountain-ringed basin . . . The Lime Kiln station is at the bottom of the grade twelve miles from Bodie and twenty and one-half from the Mills. Its elevation is 1600 feet lower than that of the Bodie end of the road.

From this point on, the track runs over a compara- tively level plain, once evidently the bed of the lake, which must have been a vast body of water, judging from the water marks on the sides of the surrounding hills and mountains.

About five miles from the Mills is a station, opposite the steamboat landing, at which are the Warm Springs. Here the little steamboat *Rocket* has been hauled up on shore . . .

By the time of my arrival in 1908, the *Rocket* had not been seen on the lake for nearly 25 years. Built in San Francisco in 1879,* it was used for a short time on San Francisco Bay and was then shipped by rail to Carson City and from there to Mono Lake, a distance of 120 miles, by team. Jim Cain bought the boat and used it for hauling wood and lumber on the lake. When the railroad was built, the company bought the steamer and used it to haul rails, locomotives, cars, sawmill equipment,

---

*Official number 110395, length 32 feet, breadth 8 feet, depth 3.8 feet, gross tonnage 5.56, horsepower, 12.—*List of Merchant Vessels of the United States, 1885.*

and other heavy loads across the lake during construction of the road from Mono Saw Mill to Bodie.

[At] Warm Springs Station on the eastern shore of Mono Lake . . . are located two or three warm springs, one of which is very large and throws out a large quantity of water. The water is possessed of mineral qualities and is soft and pleasant. Surrounding the springs are several acres of grass land. The view on every side is very picturesque and pleasing to the eye. To the west the lake stretches out, and beyond are the high peaks of the Sierra. On the south several extinct volcanoes loom up in solemn line, while the green outlines of the timber belt add renewed beauty to the landscape. On the east are rolling hills and the northern prospect opens with a monotonous flat to the hills that form the northern wall of the great Mono Lake Basin . . .

In ten miles and a quarter [from Warm Springs] the timber is reached and the sweet odor of pine and the aroma of fresh sawdust reminds one that he is a long way from Bodie. Here everything is life and activity and quite a little town has sprung up.

As surveyed and built, the distance of the railroad was 31.74 miles from Bodie station to Mono Saw Mills. Sidings were located at the terminal and at Warm Springs — eleven miles north of Mono Mills — and at Lime Kiln — twelve miles south of Bodie station. Elevations were 8500 feet at Bodie station, 6426 at Warm Springs, and 7346 at Mono Mills.

The company maintained machine and blacksmith shops at Mono Mills as well as a commissary and boarding houses there and at the logging camp and Bodie terminal during the operating season.

ix. Reconnaissance

In June 1908 Mark Kerr sent word that he was coming to Bodie with R. P. McLaughlin and for me to arrange for the necessary horses, wagon and supplies for a reconnaissance trip over the survey line of the proposed standard gauge railroad to Sodaville. This was to be in preparation for a trip to follow later with railroad people and others who were considering the possibilities for such a railroad.

McLaughlin had been in charge of the survey crews and they wanted to refresh their memories of the route surveyed. We left Mono Mills, loading the wagon, five horses, saddles, supplies, a barrel of water and feed for the horses on a flatcar coupled to the train bound for Bodie. Horses, wagon and the rest were unloaded at Lime Kiln siding. I brought along an Indian named Jake Gilbert as guide and helper, for he claimed to know the section and the waterholes en route.

The survey line actually started from Warm Springs, on the east side of Mono Lake, and across Mono Basin, but we started from Lime Kiln, thinking to eliminate a long ride across the basin where there was neither road nor water. The poorly defined road we followed had been used for hauling piñon pine wood from nearby hills. It was a sandy, volcanic road, pretty tough going for the team hauling the wagon, which we had to abandon after four or five miles. We transferred the supplies to the horses and continued on foot and saddle.

The first night we stopped near an alkali waterhole. The water was so bad that we had to resort to our meager supply in cans. The horses finally drank some of the water from the hole, but only because we had nothing else to offer. We started early the next morning to pick up the survey line at the pass to the south. Part of the survey had been made the previous year in the winter when there was snow on the ground. The stakes were hard to find and we had trouble getting our bearings. This caused considerable delay, but we finally made our way through to Whisky Flat and a well which proved more than welcome. We were nearly out of water and the horses were in bad shape.

That night we camped in Rattlesnake Canyon, near the old Garfield District. We made a waterhole, but were now almost without food and feed for the animals. We had canned tomatoes for dinner and I fed the horses a small portion of grain from my hat to prevent waste. The following afternoon we reached Sodaville, where we stopped at the old Stewart Hotel. We were very glad to get there and the Indian and I remained a couple of days to get the horses and ourselves rested, while Kerr and McLaughlin went on to Tonopah by train.

We made the return trip in better time, cutting across country in the general direction of the place where we had left the wagon. That night we camped in the hills. The Indian was sure we were going on the best route, but we had rough going the following morning, running into a box canyon. It was late in the afternoon when we reached the wagon and began the slow trip to Lime Kiln.

From Sodaville I had sent a message to Bodie, via Hawthorne, to have a train meet us at the Lime Kiln siding. We expected to be there in the afternoon, but it was midnight before we arrived and loaded the wagon, horses and gear on the cars for the return trip to Mono Mills. The train crew had just about decided we would not get there and was preparing to leave without us.

A trip from the junction of Highway 395, near Mono Lake, over the "Pole Line Road" to Hawthorne, Nevada, is now a matter of an hour's time, compared with the "roadless" trip of several days that was necessary in those times.

A short time later I made another trip with Nat Smith, who had been on the survey party. This time we started from Warm Springs and found the pass that had been surveyed, but which we had missed on the previous trip.

x. Inspection tour

In August, 1909, Charles E. Knox, president of our company brought a party of gentlemen to inspect the lumber company property and to tour the surrounding country to look over the possibilities, such as tonnage, for the proposed road. In addition to the timberlands of the company, arrangements were tentatively made with the United States Government for the purchase of forty million board feet on a stumpage basis at five dollars per thousand board feet.

In this party, besides Mr. Knox, were Mark B. Kerr, R. H. Hamlin the general manager of the Tonopah & Goldfield Railroad, a Mr. Kent representing Philadelphia interests, and two other gentlemen besides my old friend John M. Peters and myself. The others came to Bodie from Tonopah and Hawthorne in two automobiles, Thomas and Simplex seven-passenger touring cars, both chain-driven. At Bodie the cars were loaded on flatcars for the trip to Mono Mills where accommodations had been prepared for the party.

Next morning, in the automobiles, the guests started the trip through the timber to Dead Man Creek, near the Thompson Ranch in upper Long Valley. The creek was too high to ford, but two timbers placed across the stream made it possible for us to guide the autos across, the passengers having walked across beforehand.

After a stop at Mammoth, we began our return trip to Mono Mills by way of the steep, narrow Dead Man Grade, now part of Highway 395. Sand and loose volcanic material made traction very difficult and at times the passengers had to get out and push the cars up the long grade. Someone suggested that a refund was due for the high-class help needed to push the cars that had been hired at the rate of $100 a day each, the prevailing rate in Tonopah and Goldfield.

Back at Mono Mills, the automobiles were loaded on the railroad cars for the return trip to Bodie. Some of the guests rode the train, while the others remained for the horseback trip over the proposed railroad route to Sodaville.

This trip began by train from Mono Mills to Warm Springs. Here the horses and equipment were unloaded and the party proceeded to a camp that had been established about ten miles east of Mono Lake. Feed and water for the stock, and supplies and equipment for the men had previously been hauled there by a four-horse team.

The next morning the riders tied down their bedding and utensils on their saddles and the pack animals carried supplies and feed for the stock. There were no roads until the party reached Whiskey Flat. We stopped for the night at Qualey's

Excelsior copper mine. It was not operating at the time and arrangements had been made for the use of the mine's boarding house for this stop.

The following day the party continued over a trail through Rattlesnake Canyon to Garfield, where the two hired automobiles that had come from Bodie by way of Hawthorne were now waiting to take the party on to Sodaville and Tonopah. Peters and I returned to Mono Mills with the horses and pack animals, taking two days for the trip.

As it turned out, the proposed broad gauge railroad to Sodaville was never built. The old narrow gauge line continued its isolated run between Bodie and Mono Mills. Deliveries were made from Bodie to such places as Aurora, Lucky Boy and Masonic, using teams of from six to twenty animals depending on the loads, much as they had been made during the early operations.

xi. Equipment

The railroad's equipment consisted of wood-burning locomotives, three of the Mogul type with 14 x 16 inch cylinders, and one four-coupled 0-4-2T with saddle tank and 12 x 16 inch cylinders. The locomotives had been built in 1880 by the Union Iron Works in San Francisco.

Instead of numbers, the engines bore the names MONO, INYO, TYBO and BODIE. The MONO and INYO had originally been 0-6-0s and were later fitted with two-wheel "pony" trucks to overcome their tendency to climb the rails on short curves. Some years before the road was dismantled the TYBO was sold and moved to Keeler, California, where it was used at the salt plant.

When I came to work on the railroad we found the locomotives in poor condition and in the years from 1908 to 1911 considerable work was done to rehabilitate them. They were practically rebuilt with new driving boxes, brasses, bushings and what not to get them in decent running condition.

The flanges on the drivers were so worn away that they were climbing the rails. The tires had to be cut down and our shop at Mono Mills had no lathe big enough to do the work. We shipped the drivers by freight teams to Carson City where the Virginia & Truckee Railroad's machine shop was equipped to handle the job.

The locomotives had no brakes except the hand brake on the tender. Steam jams were added as were modern lubricators and injectors to replace the old "tallow pots" on the steam chests and water pumps driven from the crossheads. The steam jam worked the brake shoes only on the rear drivers of the loco- motives and on all the wheels of the tenders.

There were thirty flatcars, a tank car, five logging cars, two pole cars and a caboose, all equipped with link-and-pin coup- lings. The flatcars and logging cars were equipped with hand brakes only.

We were fortunate in having a first class machinist. Bill Jones had formerly been with the Southern Pacific shops at Sparks, Nevada. We also had an excellent blacksmith and mechanic, Gus Hess, who stayed with the company to the end.

Through the efforts and ingenuity of men like these, it was possible to keep antique equipment running for years after it would have been retired by any other railroad, and running with a pretty good safety record, too.

xii. Operations

The train leaving Mono Saw Mills would consist of ten or twelve cars of lumber and wood. One locomotive would haul it to Lime Kiln station. From there to Bodie, because of heavy grades, no more than three to four cars could be hauled at a time, depending on the loads.

On down grades the brakeman practically controlled the train with the fireman assisting him in braking on the cars. When the train gained too much momentum, they would climb over the loads to apply the brakes from car to car and back again, releasing them for flat places and light grades. The engi- neer used the "johnson bar" in reverse to help control the speed and to stop the train for lack of braking power.

The fireman had his work cut out for him on steep upgrades and had to coordinate his firing with the engineer to conserve water as well as to maintain steam pressure. The tenders were loaded with wood for fuel at the terminals and replenished at Lime Kiln station from cars of wood hauled there for the purpose.

Water supply was always a problem as there were no tanks between the Mono Mills and Bodie terminals. It was necessary to fill the boiler of the locomotive to capacity and the tender at the overflow point before leaving Mono Mills with the loaded train. Then it required careful use of the water to avoid having to leave the loads and run for the water tank near Bodie to replenish the supply before backing again to where the loaded cars had been left.

The railroad never collected any passenger fares. If permission for a ride on the trains was granted, it was with the understanding that the person did so at his or her own risk, riding on the flatcars or on top of the lumber or cordwood en route to the Bodie terminal. Needless to say, no timetable was ever issued.

xiii. Difficult winter trip

Trips could be very difficult, particularly in the fall and winter when working with reduced crews and before the railroad was all snowed in. Once in December 1910 it took five days to complete the 32 miles from Mono Mills to Bodie. This train consisted of an engine with a V-type snowplow on the pilot, a car of fuel wood for the Lime Kiln station and two flatcars loaded with a gasoline engine and other equipment to be transferred to Bodie.

The first day a car jumped the track and the train had to return to the Mills. The next day trouble came a few miles north of Lime Kiln where the snow drifts were so deep that it was late afternoon before the train reached the high trestle eight miles from Bodie. From here on it was a case of bucking snow until the steam pressure dropped, shoveling snow into the tender to be melted by steam to provide more water for the boiler, then back again to bucking snow which became ever deeper as the train climbed the grade.

About midnight the one car still coupled to the engine jumped the track and had to be dropped, for it had begun to slide down the side of the canyon. The thermometer read twenty below zero and the four-man crew and two passengers huddled about the boiler in the engine cab to thaw out. When pressure dropped the engine stopped and out they would climb to clear the track, shovel snow into the tender and hunt for old ties under the snow for fuel. Ten minutes after leaving the cab their clothes would be frozen stiff.

By two in the morning the engine was completely stalled in a deep drift, four miles from the Bodie terminal. Now we had to make our way on foot, taking turns breaking a trail through the waist-deep snow. Everyone was exhausted on reaching the terminal office. It took three more days to work the engine into the roundhouse. Water and fuel had to be hauled to it by sleigh and additional help was needed for clearing the track.

xiv. Springtime reopening

During the winter it was necessary to deliver lumber and wood to the Bodie area. Breaking out a road in the snow and keeping it open was bad enough, but when you had to leave the road to pull into a yard, the real trouble began.

As the winter approached its end there would be special difficulties as the snow began to melt a bit during the day, then froze up nights. After dark a team with a sleighload of lumber or wood could travel over the crusted snow with little trouble, but shortly after sunrise it became impassable as the ice crust quickly melted. Consequently, during the early spring most deliveries were made between midnight and sunrise.

When the time came to open the railroad for the season, sleighs would be loaded with fine dirt from the mine dumps, the darker the better. Teams would be hitched up long before dawn, and driven along the line of the railroad track while men walked alongside of the sleigh, sprinkling the dirt like salt on the snow which covered the track. This was often done for a distance of four miles in the early morning hours over the crusted snow so it would be possible to return to the stables before sunrise. The sun's heat would be absorbed by the dark dirt, causing the snow to melt faster. This made a difference of three to four feet, clearing the track while the snow not so treated remained banked on either side.

During the early spring, while there were still stretches of track covered with snow, it was sometimes possible for us to get the rail motor speedster from Bodie to Mono Mills by carrying along a pair of portable ten-foot sections of wooden track. When we came to a patch of snow, we would put one of these on the snow and push the car on it, and from it to the other section, over and over to the next clear track. This was strenuous work that we avoided as much as possible.

xv. Mono Mills

The sawmills at the southern end of the railroad cut the fine Jeffrey pine timber which the railroad carried to Bodie. The impressions of the journalist who visited Mono Mills in 1882 were similar to my own:

The saw mill, being the chief object of interest to a new arrival, the reporter immediately proceeded to inspect the machinery and its general workings. This is a large and well equipped mill — one of the best on the coast. It is located about five miles and a quarter from the bank of the lake in a small ravine. The upper story of the building is on a level with the surrounding country, so there is no trouble whatever in rolling the logs into the mill.

The logs are first passed through the upper and lower saws, which are fifty-four inches in size . . . There are three other saws in the mill — one being a forty-four inch pony, and two cut-off saws . . .

The machinery of the mill is propelled by an engine with a sixteen inch cylinder . . . These saws have a capacity of turning out 80,000 feet of lumber every ten hours

. . . The water supply is brought from springs in a two inch pipe and there is enough for all practical purposes . . .

The company's lumber tract embraces 12,000 acres and some of it is covered with immense pine . . . From the mill site a very pretty view can be obtained of the lake, and altogether the location is inviting.[*]

The sawmill came in for considerable repair between 1908 and 1911 and about 1910 a four-saw edger was added. The mill had the usual skidways for the lumber and the logs were unloaded from the trains at a dry landing.

xvi. Labor

In 1908 the lumber company paid common labor three dollars for a ten-hour day, seven a.m. to six p.m. with an hour off for lunch. Locomotive engineers received five dollars a day, firemen and brakemen, four; the head sawyer in the mill earned six dollars a day. Quarters in bunkhouses or other types of structure were free at Mono Mills; a dollar a day bought three meals of board. The ranchers who delivered sides of beef to Mono Mills received ten cents a pound for the meat. All payment was in cash.

Capable and skilled laborers were at a premium in Bodie; unemployment among them was at a minimum. In event of illness or a man quitting his job, it was almost impossible to replace a locomotive engineer, mill sawyer or jerkline teamster, for example, without considerable loss of time. As a result the railroad and lumber company often had to press skilled men into jobs foreign to them and quite different from their usual work.

A locomotive engineer might have to double as a jerkline teamster hauling logs from the timber to the logging landing. A storekeeper might be found operating a locomotive. A machinist or blacksmith might find himself filling another position. All this was done without argument or complaint as this was a time for flexibility. In my own case, I filled in as an engineer, sawyer and almost everything else.

----
[*]*Weekly Standard News,* October 12, 1881

xvii. Emergencies

There were many narrow escapes from serious injury. Logging cars were derailed or broke in two under heavy loads. Runaway cars loaded with lumber sometimes caused trouble. The railroad, logging and sawmill operations were full of hazards and we had our share of accidents; an emergency kit was kept ready. We were fortunate that, as far as I can learn, there was never a fatality during the construction of the railroad or all the long years of these operations.

When medical attention was required at Mono Mills or in the timber area, ingenuity had to prevail. In the most extreme emergencies the doctor was available in Bodie, but that was 32 miles away and when emergency treatment was required, necessity became the mother of invention.

One such case occurred early one spring when four of us went from Bodie to Mono Mills on one of those exhausting trips when we had to use the portable track sections to get over innumerable patches of snow on the tracks. One of us was a young man, Kurt Schmidt, newly arrived from Europe, who worked hard and made no complaint of not feeling well. The morning after our arrival at the Mills he complained of a severe headache and a high fever and said he had had no bowel movement for several days. It was out of the question to return to Bodie by the speedster and the trip would take two days by team and wagon.

The case called for immediate action and with the doctor 32 miles north of us, we conferred and decided that he needed an enema. Lacking the necessary equipment, we looked around the bar and soon found suitable substitutes. A small rubber tube which had been used for siphoning wine from barrels into bottles was put through the cork of a gallon demijohn, which made an admirable reservoir for the occasion. One of the boys stood on a chair to hold this high. The remedy was successful and the patient quickly recovered.

In the most extreme emergencies, particularly when the tracks were clear, the doctor could be brought to Mono Mills, but generally the patient was brought to him to save time. The following incident illustrates the necessity of this.

Late one fall, after the railroad and sawmill had been closed for the season, three or four Indians were still at Mono Mills hunting. A young Indian named China Willie, for some unexplained reason, shot Lefty Jack, another Indian, with a .22 rifle. The caretaker at the Mills store, hearing of the shooting, dressed the wound as best he could, but was not able to remove the bullet. He telephoned our Bodie office and asked that the doctor come to the Mills.

With Dr. Ware, Stuart Cain and another man, I came on the speedster, an Oldsmobile that had just been converted to rail use. There were still a number of "bugs" to be worked out in this vehicle, but since it was the only available transportation we took a chance on it. The trip from Bodie was accomplished with little trouble and at the Mills the doctor attended the Indian and removed the bullet. Jack recovered, none the worse for the target practice, and appreciated the doctor's services.

Meanwhile, the trip back to Bodie was not as successful as the trip out. The night was cold but fortunately we all had heavy coats. Halfway to Bodie the motor quit, for the dry batteries supplying power for the ignition system were exhausted. We had to walk four miles to Lime Kiln siding where there was a telephone in a small cabin that connected with the line from Mono Mills to Bodie.

It was midnight and repeated ringing of the phone brought no answer from the clerk who lived in the Bodie office building. As there was no chance to get new batteries sent out with a team that night, Stuart Cain and I stayed in the cabin. There was no stove, but we found a five gallon oil can and built a fire in it to provide some heat. Meanwhile, the doctor and his assistant decided to walk the remaining ten miles to Bodie, mostly uphill through the brush. It was a tough walk they later admitted.

The next morning we managed to get a response to our repeated phone calls; the clerk said he had not heard the phone ringing during the night. He agreed to bring us six new dry batteries, but it was a slow trip for him with a team and buggy over a road seldom used. It was noon before he arrived at the cabin. He took us to the motorcar where we installed the new batteries and had no further trouble finishing the trip to Bodie. The one-way trip from Mono Mills had this time taken 24 hours.

Another time, an Indian was trying to clear his shotgun of a shell that was stuck in the gun. Foolishly he placed a rod in the barrel and pounded on it to remove the shell. It certainly did, with the result that his right hand was badly mangled, with three fingers hanging loosely by the skin.

He walked from his shack to the store at the Mills for help. At the time my brother and I were the only ones there and we promptly placed his hand in a basin of warm water with a Lysol solution. It was very painful to the Indian and this was one time where there was no doubt that he needed a good stiff drink of whiskey to keep him on his feet.

We bandaged the hand the best we could and then I took him to Bodie on the motorcar. There he walked down the hill with me to the doctor's residence The doctor took one look at the hand and snipped the skin holding the three fingers, then he sewed and bandaged the hand without a whimper from the Indian.

The hand healed quickly and he was back to work in a short time.

Through the years, Bodie's post office has moved to a number of places. When I arrived in 1908 it was in the building at the right of the view above, on the west side of Main Street. By 1912 it had moved two doors south to the Reading store, the third building from the right. Between the two buildings was "Burkham's, the Store of Quality." My first nights in Bodie were spent in Nate Boyd's Occidental Hotel on the east side of Main Street.

The office building at the Bodie railroad yard on the hill, above, was my headquarters. The storm entrance is at the right. The hilltop reservoir is still there. When I took the lower picture in 1936, after most of Bodie's population was gone, we were kidding the mine manager by pretending to be fishing in the reservoir which he had stocked with fish for his own sport. In the picture are members of the Cain family and, at the right, my brother Gus.

The two views show the railroad and lumber yard on the hill above
Bodie. It looks like a valley in the picture, but actually was a half-mile
climb above the town. The superintendent of the nearby Lent shaft used
that house. I took the upper picture in about 1909, as the INYO pushed
cars loaded with cordwood to the woodpile. Somebody took the lower
picture of me, a couple of years later, when the piles were bigger. The
water tank, visible over the lumber pile at the right, was no longer in use
by then; we had a newer one half a mile down the track near the Red
Cloud shaft. The Summit mine is on top of the hill.

This picture, from the Cain family collection, shows the Bodie lumber
yard in about 1880, before the railroad was built.

The top picture, opposite, shows me at Adobe Meadows on the way to Benton, the village shown in the two views under it. The little town was beautifully situated on a wooded meadow at the foot of the White Mountains. The water there is very good, but so hot that you have to cool it before you can drink it. The place is now called Benton Hot Springs; the town now labeled "Benton" on the maps, we knew as Benton Station on the old narrow gauge Carson & Colorado railroad. Above is our Oldsmobile speedster with Gus Hess at the wheel and Ed Stinson in front. It is at Bodie, loaded with supplies for Mono Mills. Below is the Inyo and our blocky wooden tank car at Mono Mills. (*Opposite bottom, Frasher's Fotos, Pomona, Calif.*)

We had "piggyback cars" more than fifty years ago! That was how Mr. Knox and his inspection party got the automobiles they had rented at $100 a day from Bodie to Mono Mills. The engine watering up, below, is the MONO.

The saddle-tanker, above, is the BODIE. Below is the 260-foot trestle between Bodie and Lime Kiln. At the bottom of the page, the INYO hauls a string of log cars over the shorter trestle near Mono Mills.

At the wheel of the Oldsmobile speedster, at the top of the opposite page, is Gus Hess and his brother Will behind him with the dogs. I'm wearing my sheep-lined coat and we're about to leave the woodpile at Mono Mills to go duck shooting by Mono Lake. In the middle picture, the MONO works up the grade into Bodie yard. The bottom picture opposite and top one on this page show that engine with a string of empties negotiating the switchback on the way to the Mills. Our first speedster, below, was homemade and driven by a two-cycle air-cooled engine. On it, in Bodie yard, are Lester Bell and George Denham; I am standing out in front.

Here is the BODIE, a saddle-tanker, on the job at Mono Mills. Finished lumber emerged from the mill on the skidway, below. In the winter scene, top opposite, is the MONO by the shop at the Mills, the same building which appears in the middle picture with the INYO wooded up for the haul to Bodie; the Mono Craters are in the background. At the bottom, the same engine hauls a cabin to the Lime Kiln siding.

Here is how the turntable looked underneath. When the picture was taken in 1909 we were installing a new one at Mono Mills. Look at the size of those logs the Mono is delivering to the skidway at the Mills! They weren't all that big.

This trainload of giant logs is being delivered to the mill by MONO. The
INYO, below, is working at the log landing in the woods. We made that
donkey engine at the left from an assortment of spare and salvaged parts.

Not all the logging was done by railroad. Here is one of those solid wheeled logging wagons drawn by an eight-horse jerk-line team, driven by a teamster mounted on the near wheel-horse. Below, the logs are dragged with the aid of Michigan wheels.

The boarding house at Mono Mills, above, had a handy locomotive bell on the porch roof to announce meal times. The Mono Mills store was right by the railroad track. On the porch, below, is Nat Smith, by the door; the man on the tender with the suspenders is Walter Farrington.

All the mining and milling activities of the Standard Mining Co. came to their conclusion with the pouring of a bullion bar in the melting room.

CHAPTER THREE

MINING IN THE MONO LAKE REGION

i. Old-time mining

Bodie's fame as a brawling frontier camp of the Wild West would not have been possible without the solid mining achievements that attracted thousands of people in the late 1870s and early 1880s. The Bodie Mining District was discovered in 1859 by William S. Bodey of Poughkeepsie, New York, who with three companions crossed over the Sierra from Sonora to the Mono Lake region on a prospecting trip that brought them to the site of what became Bodie. After discovering placer gold, Bodey and his partners are believed to have established their camp near the Pearson Spring just west of the present townsite. Their efforts met with scant success, for there was little water available for their purpose, and after Bodey's death during a severe snowstorm in the winter of 1859-1860, his partners left for other fields.

The camp became known to a few prospectors and they organized the mining district there on July 10, 1860, naming it after the discoverer, William S. Bodey. It is said that the spelling of the name was changed to Bodie through the mistake of a careless sign painter. A year later the Bunker Hill Lode, now a part of the Standard Mining Co. property was discovered. In the fall of 1863 a number of the Bodie mining companies consolidated their claims which, with mill sites, tunnel sites and so on, were purchased by the Empire Mill & Mining Co. of New York. For a short period there was considerable excitement followed by failure of the enterprise and the district was abandoned for three or four years by all but a few optimistic prospectors.

In 1872 some very rich ore was found in the Bullion location and it was mined by the owners who milled their ores in arrastras, or stone grinding mills, at Rough Creek five miles northeast of Bodie. This mill was purchased in 1876 by San Francisco capitalists and, with associated mining claims, became the Standard Mine. The operations of this company in 1878 resulted in the discovery of exceedingly rich quartz ore in the extension of two of the Standard veins found in the Bodie Mine, adjoining the Standard to the south. The rush was soon on from everywhere and excitement was high; population mushroomed to an estimated 10,000 people in 1878-1881.

Jim Cain told me that during the height of the boom, when the Bodie Mine was in operation, they had a ten-stamp mill with pan amalgamation. The ore came from the Fortuna vein on the 400-foot level and was very rich. Gold and silver filled the battery until the stamps could no longer crush the ore. The mill men removed the gold and silver grindings from the battery, dried them and melted the metal into bullion with no further treatment. They milled a thousand tons, averaging $640 a ton from the Bodie Mine and another thousand from the Bulwer Mine that averaged $240 a ton.

Several mills in the district operated a total of 180 stamps in the treatment of mine ores. Bodie Mill operated sixty, the Noonday Mill operated forty, and twenty each were operated by the Syndicate, Standard, Bullwer and Bodie Tunnel mills.

A period of slow decline followed the boom, assisted by the failure of the Noonday and Red Cloud companies on which J. B. Haggin and George Hearst foreclosed for $540,000 in November 1882. By the following year all but the larger mines stopped work and the population of Bodie dwindled. Between forty and fifty mines and mills had been in operation during the three boom years; after September 1888 there were about three.

Operating costs were very high in the early days and records indicate that ore running less than $12 a ton could not be handled at a profit with the pan amalgamation or plate and vanner processes, with which recovery was low. The lower grade ores went into the mine dumps. The result was a high grade mill product and high grade tailings, that at first were allowed to flow down Bodie Creek to be deposited on fields and other property along the banks for many miles below Bodie. Ranchers and property owners complained bitterly about the debris until a new development changed their attitude.

ii. Technological advance

The advent of the cyanide process for the recovery of gold and silver was pioneered in Bodie about 1890. This made it possible to leach the tailings profitably and property owners down the creek built small cyanide leaching plants to treat the tailings on their land. A profitable crop of gold and silver bullion, more valuable than hay and vegetables, changed the deposits of tailings and debris from a curse to a blessing.

At various times there were five different plants along the creek for the treatment of tailings. One of them was 15 miles below Bodie. Trouble developed between the mining companies and ranchers and eventually the tailings were held back by the construction of dams below the mills.

The Standard Mill was destroyed by fire in 1896. The company cleared up the debris and rebuilt the mill, which is still standing on the same site. It is reported that gold and silver recovered in the cleanup of the old mill produced sufficient money to cover the cost of the new mill.

In 1905 a slimes plant was erected and began treating the accumulated tailings from the tailing ponds and from the Standard Mill. This brought extraction up to about ninety per cent. From this operation the company realized a large sum of money that helped it to maintain operations for many years longer than would otherwise have been possible.

The other big economic change that benefited Bodie's mines during the 1890s was the advent of electric power which greatly reduced the cost of pumping water from the lower levels. Before the beginning of service from the Green Creek dynamo, the high cost of wood fuel for steam made water removal very costly. The Cornish type pump used at the Lent shaft, for example, was an immense machine. It averaged 7½ strokes a minute and threw forty gallons of water with each stroke, about 300 gallons a minute. Besides these pumps, some mines used large buckets running up and down the shaft. Electric power brought the cost of this operation within reason.

Many able and prominent men spent a part of their lives in Bodie. Theodore Hoover was general manager of the Standard Mining Co. Later he went to Stanford University where he headed the School of Mines. His famous brother, Herbert Hoover, came to visit him in Bodie and stayed in the building behind the Standard Mill that is now known as the Hoover residence.

Thomas H. Leggett, a noted mining engineer was in charge of the Standard Mining Co. when, in the early 1890s, the Green Creek power plant was installed with its unprecedented 13-mile transmission line. He became so well known for this achievement that he was subsequently engaged to direct mining projects at many other locations in the United States and abroad.

Paul M. Downing, an electrician, later became vice president and general manager of the Pacific Gas & Electric Co. in San Francisco.

Charles Merrill, a chemist, designed the cyanide plant which proved a great success and made profitable the reworking of tailings from the mining activities of Bodie's boom years, bringing the camp a new and much more sustained era of prosperity.

It was during this new prosperity in the old camp that I arrived on the scene to work on the railroad. The camp was dominated physically and economically by the mines. The most conspicuous structure in the place was the formidable complex of corrugated iron buildings belonging to the Standard Mining Co., with the long tramway leading to the mill on the mountain east of Main Street. All activity in Bodie was connected in one way or another with the operation of the mines. Without them, of course, there would have been no Bodie.

Gold production in the Bodie Mining District has amounted to a total value of from 75 to 100 millions of dollars over the years. The records on which this estimate is based are incomplete, but the best available. The ore deposits are extensive and in 1912 it was reported that the Standard Mining Co. was working on some 35 different veins, averaging about three feet in width. Some are but a few inches wide, while the main Standard vein is about twenty feet in width. The Lent shaft, at 1200 feet, is the deepest in the camp.

iii. Wages

When I came to Bodie the mining companies were paying wages on much the same basis as was the lumber company. Common outside labor earned three dollars for a ten hour day without coffee break. Miners earned four dollars for a nine hour day that was later reduced to eight hours.

At these rates the men could meet the hotels' going price of $35 a month for room and board, three meals a day, and still have money for the whiskey that sold at two drinks for a quarter in the saloons, and for gambling or such other recreational opportunities as the camp offered.

"High-grading," the stealing of rich ores from the mines was common in Bodie as it was in other mining camps. It was overcome, to some extent, by the installation of "change rooms" where the miners had to change into working clothes before entering the mine and back to street clothes at the end of their shift. This did not entirely solve the management's problem, for dinner buckets and other means still remained as tempting ways to smuggle high grade ores out of a mine.

iv. Jim Cain, man of the West

No history of Bodie is complete without prominent mention of James Stuart Cain, a businessman who arrived in the midst of the first big boom in 1879 and did not leave until after the fire that destroyed most of the business district in 1932.

He was a Canadian, born in 1854 at Rockburn, Quebec near the New York state line. In 1875 he went to Carson City,

Nevada, where he met Martha Delilah Wells, a resident of nearby Genoa, Nevada's first white settlement. Her uncle was governor of Utah territory where she was born. In 1879 they were married and moved to Bodie early in the big boom.

Jim went into the lumber business there and concerned himself with the freighting of badly-needed timber products and supplies to the bustling mining camp on its treeless flat. He acquired barges and used the tiny steamer *Rocket* to haul lumber across Mono Lake. He transported the survey party for the Bodie Railway & Lumber Co. across the lake from Warford Springs on the north toward a landing on the south shore. While they were on the lake a wild storm blew up and made it almost impossible for the sixty-foot scow, loaded with horses, wagons and equipment, to gain headway. Jim Cain acted as captain, but became sick on the rough voyage. By nightfall the party had reached the south shore where they all slept in a haystack. The next day they continued seven miles south to the timber where they selected the site for Mono Mills. On the way back, Jim sold the steamer and scow to the lumber company. He had had enough of the lake.

During the next few years Jim made some rather fortunate mining strikes and in 1888 he purchased a half-interest in the bank. Four years later he bought the other half and continued to operate the bank for the next forty years. It served as headquarters for his other business operations. He was agent for the Wells, Fargo & Co. express until 1912, when service was discontinued and Bodie had to depend on the parcel post.

The Cains had four children: David Victor, Jessie Delilah (Dolly), James Isaac (Jimmy) and Stuart Wells. Dolly attended Mills College in Oakland and was an excellent pianist. After returning to Bodie she assisted for a time in her father's bank and then went to Aurora where she worked in the store and was later appointed assistant postmaster. After a year or so there, she returned to Bodie.

I met her at a dance in 1909 at the Miners Union Hall and during the following months we often attend social gatherings together. I also visited her frequently at the Cain home. On

October 7, 1911, the sixth anniversary of my departure from New York, we were married in San Francisco. In Bodie we purchased the Donnelly house on the west side of town, near her father's house. Ours was the only green spot in town. Hops covered the front and sides of our house; no other green plant could survive in Bodie's harsh climate.

Jim Cain acquired the Standard Mining Co. property in 1915. He was confident that Bodie would eventually return to prosperity, particularly after it was demonstrated that a large tonnage of workable ore in the mine dumps and surface ground of the Standard property could be treated at a profit. He kept this faith, even after his bank and other property were destroyed by fire. In the later years he and his wife came to San Francisco to live with Dolly and me. He died October 28, 1936, his wife, April 25, 1943.

Jim Cain's hope must be further deferred, since 1942 when operations were closed under the "gold clause," until there is a change in economic conditions and a justified rise in the price of gold for the mining industry.

v. Peter's "millun dollar" claim

An old miner whose first name was Peter had a mining claim he called the Charleston, located at the southern end of the Bodie District, near the railroad track for Mono Mills. Although he had held this claim for some years, he never worked it except to do the annual assessment work the law required to hold a mining claim. He generally did this work during the summer or fall season.

Nearly every morning then he would be seen walking by the railroad office with his lunch bucket. One of the men in the lumber yard would greet him, "Good morning, Peter, where are you going?" The answer would always be the same, "To the Charleston, if you please." He had never found any ore, but he continued to hold onto the claim nevertheless.

Eventually, Peter was taken ill and had to be moved to the county hospital near Bridgeport and his brother was notified of the illness. The brother arrived to see what he could do to help.

Peter, however, was a proud man and would accept nothing that smacked of charity, even from his brother. The situation was difficult.

The brother asked Sheriff Bert Dolan to help him, suggesting that the officer, whom Peter knew well, find out if the old man would sell his mining claim. The brother had agreed to give a thousand dollars to be turned over to Peter for the claim, which was worthless, but this seemed a promising way to overcome his objection to outside help.

The sheriff approached Peter on the proposed deal, asking what he thought the mining claim was worth, as he might have a buyer at a reasonable price. Expecting an answer of a couple of hundred dollars at the most, the sheriff was greatly surprised when Peter said, hopefully, "Would a *millun* be too much?"

No deal could be worked out with Peter for less than that figure and his brother had to arrange for assistance to him in another way.

vi.   Leasers work the mines

High on the hill above the lumber yard was the Standard Mine hoist. Lumber and heavy timber for the mine had to be hauled on wagons with four-horse teams, up a heavy grade with a switchback and a sharp turn at the top, passing near the Summit Mine dump. Once, about 1912, a lumber company team came upon a dead man lying on the road near this dump. The teamster stopped to investigate and found that this was the body of Alex Ross, a miner who for some time had been working, under lease, a quartz vein that came to the surface at that point. Nearby was a sharp rock, the size of a fist and covered with blood. It turned out that Ross had been blasting. His custom, after lighting the fuse, was to go to the south side of the dump, which was over twenty feet high, for shelter from the flying rock and dirt thrown out by the blast when it came. This time he had not made it to safety.

Leasers, independent miners like Alex Ross, who worked portions of mine properties owned by other people or companies, became more common in Bodie following the closing of Standard Mining Co. operations when that firm's properties were acquired in 1915 by Jim Cain and associates. The operations had gone on continuously for decades and their discontinuance was followed by a noticeable drop in Bodie's small population. For several years considerable ore was produced by miners who leased blocks of ground in these properties from the Cain Company, which treated the ores in the Standard mill and shipped the bullion to the San Francisco Mint. Very few of the leasers suffered the unfortunate fate that befell Alex Ross.

During this period a group of us tried our luck in several places at various times. One such lease was in the New Standard tunnel. We were certain that the veins we sought would be found, but it was a question of their value and size when we did find them.

We ran the tunnel ahead in very hard formation and had cut three or four veins from a foot or two in width, but the values were very low. Finally we ran a drift southerly on one of the veins that looked most promising and after about forty feet of drifting, suddenly we came to a point where a quartz feeder entered the vein, disclosing gold plastered in spots on the foot wall of the vein.

This was assayed at about $1700 per ton. It looked mighty encouraging and the news spread around the camp that we had a vein that might be the Fortuna. The Fortuna was a cross vein that had produced much high grade ore in various mines in the camp.

At about this time, I made a trip in the Adobe Meadows country, east of Mono Mills, to look at a prospect that two Indians, Frank Couch and George Washington, had asked me to inspect. They had sunk a small incline hole about 15 feet deep. On the bottom they found what they thought was high grade gold ore. We took some samples of the glittering materiel which panned like gold. I sent it away to be assayed and it turned out to be "fool's gold," of little value.

One day two of us were panning some of the high grade ore from our lease in Bodie. Seeing some of the boys from the camp coming along, we decided to see what they would make of this other stuff. So we put away the high grade ore and began panning the samples from Adobe Meadows.

A miner, Jim Glenn, passed by and saw us panning it. He knew that we had struck high grade ore and wanted to see what the panning looked like. We showed him the pan and stressed how much gold was there. He examined it carefully for awhile, then burst out, "Who are you trying to fool? Why, that's fool's gold from Adobe Meadows. I went there on a wild goose chase many years ago!"

The joke was on us and it shows that you can't fool a good old miner. Incidentally, the high grade ore we had in the lease did not hold out.

vii. Aurora Mining District

While Bodie was the most celebrated of the mining camps in the Mono Lake area, there were other camps nearby that produced fortunes in bullion at one time or another. Perhaps the best known of these was Bodie's neighbor, Aurora, about a dozen miles to the east and just over the Nevada line.

I first went to Aurora in the summer of 1908 and found less than 100 residents in the camp, which had a number of moldering brick buildings that bespoke a much more prosperous past. As a matter of fact the camp, after its discovery in 1860, had held nearly 10,000 people during the boom years of the 1860s. It was of sufficient importance then that California had designated it as seat of the then newly-organized Mono County. For three years the prosperous camp functioned in this capacity and a fine brick courthouse was built to house the county business. A dispute between California and Nevada as to the exact location of the state line was not settled until an official survey was completed in 1863, shortly after Nevada became a state. This survey placed the line to the west of Aurora, which thereby became part of Nevada. Mono County business was moved to Bridgeport and Aurora became the seat of Esmeralda County, Nevada. As the camp's fortunes dwindled the seat of Esmeralda County was moved to Goldfield and Aurora found itself part of a new county, Mineral, whose courthouse was in Hawthorne, 27 miles east.

The Cain Consolidated Mining Co., incorporated in 1905, owned most of the important mines in the district and had a small mill in operation. The mining activity was carried on by leasers.

In 1912 the Jesse Knight interests of Provo, Utah purchased the Cain mining properties in Aurora and formed the Aurora Consolidated Mining Co. This firm erected a forty-stamp mill and cyanide plant with a capacity of 500 tons a day, along with shops, warehouses, cottages and bunkhouses. The new construction was over the hill from the old town and was named Mangum after one of the new owners. Liquor was prohibited and no saloons were allowed, an interesting situation in a Nevada mining camp.

Naturally all these developments resulted in a rush of new activity in the old town of Aurora. Old buildings from previous boom years were rehabilitated and new ones erected to meet the need for stores, rooming houses, and especially saloons. To meet the needs of thirsty miners from "dry" Mangum, plenty of drinking places made their appearance, including the Hermitage Bar, Tunnel Saloon, Aurora Club, Northern, Elite Bar and the First & Last Chance Saloon.

With the revival of the district came a big demand for lumber for the new construction and remodeling necessary to meet the needs of the increased business. The Mono Lake Lumber Co. installed a planing mill in the Bodie railroad yards. Every day a string of big teams totaling some sixty animals hauled the lumber to Aurora. There a lumberyard and sheds were built on the hill with a combination office and living quarters for the company agent. This was furnished with bedroom furniture, desk, chairs, filing cabinets and other necessities.

Sometimes the agent, Ed Stinson, had to make a trip to Bodie with reports on the Aurora business. Once he stayed overnight at Bodie and returned to Aurora to find that the bedroom furniture and chairs had been removed from the building during his absence. He telephoned the news to the Bodie office and promptly I went to Aurora to investigate and report the loss to Deputy Sheriff Minton. It was our policy to keep on good terms with the public and we did not expect trouble of this nature. We told the deputy that we would offer a reward for apprehension of the culprits. He suggested that I calm down and do nothing until he had investigated. I returned to Bodie and after two days received a telephone call from Stinson. The furniture, he said, had been returned in good condition and the deputy said to forget the whole thing.

My curiosity was now aroused. On my next trip I was in Aurora only a short time when a man I knew well, one who could think up all kinds of devilment, came over to greet me. He told me he was sorry that he and his partner had caused us trouble. Had they known I was interested in the property on the hill, he said, they never would have molested it.

Under the circumstances, all I could do was to buy all of them a drink, including the deputy. We had no more trouble of this sort.

In 1914 the Goldfield Consolidated Mining Co. acquired the Aurora properties of the Knight interests and completed construction work on the plant and cottages in Mangum. This firm operated until 1917, after which the mill and buildings were dismantled and sold off. The old town soon lost most of its inhabitants and dwindled to a few people by 1920. Shortly it was completely deserted. The town was stripped of everything. Even the old brick buildings were torn down and the bricks packed off, until not a building remained standing in Aurora and there was only some debris to indicate that there had ever been a camp there.

viii. Castle Peak Mining District

The most important mine here is the Dunderberg, about 12 miles south of Bridgeport, at an elevation of about 8500 feet on the eastern slope of the Sierra. It was discovered and located by Charles Snyder & Co. about 1870, and afterwards purchased by Dr. George Munckton and others from Carson City, Nevada.

The mine was developed by a 40-foot shaft, then by two tunnels. A 20-stamp mill, powered by water, a concentration plant and chlorination and cyanide plants were in operation on the property at various times. An English syndicate acquired the property and started a tunnel from Green Creek Canyon to tap the main vein. A disastrous fire destroyed the plant and the operation was shut down.

Later, the property was acquired by the J. S. Cain Co. which sold it in 1959 to the present owner, Donald I. Segerstrom, of Sonora, California.

ix. Homer Mining District (Lundy)

This district was organized late in 1879, about six miles west of Mono Lake in an alpine setting in two of the eastern canyons of the Sierra. The principal mining activity has been confined to the south of Mill Creek Canyon and in Lake Canyon. The town of Lundy is at the western end of Lundy Lake at an elevation of about 7500 feet, in Mill Creek Canyon.

The principal mine in the district is the May Lundy, which produced most of the estimated 1.5 million dollars of the district. A mill was built by the Crystal Lake Gold Mining Co., a successor of the May Lundy, at Crystal Lake at an elevation of about 9500 feet. Not far from the mill, a tunnel was run about three quarters of a mile to cut the veins nearly 1500 feet from the outcrop.

About 1910, Charles E. Knox from Tonopah and the nationally known geologist and mining engineer, Josiah E. Spurr accompanied R. T. Pierce, manager and principal owner of the Crystal Lake Mining Co. on a trip to Lundy to examine the property. I accompanied the party from Bodie in one of the Burkham auto stages, hired for the trip. When we reached Lundy we left the automobile and continued on horseback up the steep grade to Crystal Lake mill and the adit of the tunnel.

Knox, Spurr and Pierce decided to inspect the tunnel to its face. As there was a danger of bad air in the long tunnel, they asked me, as a precaution, to remain at the entrance. If they did not return after a reasonable time I was to enter the tunnel to determine the cause of the delay. They returned to the entrance sooner than they expected, for their candles went out repeatedly in the foul air which would have incapacitated them had they tried to continue their trip. We returned to Lundy that evening and the next day made a casual examination of the Goleta Mine, also in the Jordan district, before going back to Bodie.

Several years later, Thomas Hanna, manager and owner, did considerable work and treated tailings from the early operations. In the later years the property has been idle, but the little town of Lundy and its scenery has become a tourist attraction.

John Dondero, a rancher in the Mono Lake area, was a big man who could hold a hundred-pound sack of potatoes under each arm. When he came to town to sell his farm products, carrying a couple of sacks of potatoes, someone would usually stop to engage him in conversation to see how long John could hold the sacks before proceeding on his way.

On one of his trips to Lundy, he staked his saddle horse in the small cemetery close to town, as there was a good growth of grass for his horse to feed on while John attended to his business. A couple of practical jokers thought they would have some fun with John, who did not leave town until dark. The jokers had gone ahead of him, carrying a couple of white sheets, and were waiting for him in the cemetery.

When John approached, they jumped up from behind the headstones at the graves, covered with sheets, yelling, hooting and waving their arms like a couple of ghosts. They thought they could scare him into a hasty retreat, but John was equal to the occasion. He reached for the quirt that was tied to his saddle and went after the "ghosts," lashing away and yelling, "Get back in your holes!" The jokers made a hurried exit and the joke was on them.

x. Jordan Mining District

This district, which was organized in 1879, lies about six miles northeast of Lundy on the easterly flank of the Sierra and in the northwestern section of the Mono Basin.

The principal mines are those that belonged to the Goleta Consolidated Mining Co. They are located on Copper Mountain at elevations ranging from 7000 to 9000 feet above sea level.

Most of the operations were carried on between 1894 and 1902. A 40-stamp mill was erected in 1896 for the treatment of gold- and silver-bearing ores. The mill was run by water diverted from Lundy Lake through a ditch to the mill. A small smelter was also erected not far from the present site of the electric power plant at Jordan, now the property of the Southern California Edison Co. The smelter was used for the treatment of copper and base metal ores developed in the southern part of the mine.

The property changed hands several times and was acquired by the J. S. Cain Co. in the 1930s. Considerable work was done in 1956 and 1957 in clearing up the old workings, but the property has been idle since then.

xi. Lake Mining District (Mammoth)

About 25 miles south of Mono Lake, in the heart of the Sierra, lies the Lake Mining District. Within a radius of about 15 miles from Mammoth City, at an elevation of about 8300 feet, are at least a dozen lakes.

The Mammoth Mining Co. began work on its mine in 1878 and suspended operations in late 1881. Intermittently work was carried on here and on other properties for some years thereafter. They constructed a mill that was later acquired by J. S. Cain of Bodie. Soon the mill was wrecked and the machinery and equipment hauled away. The big flywheel was the only iron left. The Cain Co. intended to break this up and ship it out before vandals could complete the job, but the United States Forest Service prevailed on them to leave the flywheel as a relic and tourist attraction.

With all its lakes and mountain scenery, Mammoth has become well known as a major winter sports and summer vacation area.

xii. Masonic Mining District

This district was founded in 1860 by prospectors from Mono Diggings, near the lake. The district was a mile and a half west of the Nevada line and 12 miles northeast of Bridgeport, in Mono County, California.

Little was attempted in the way of mining or building of a settlement in the early years, probably because of the early discoveries and extensive operations that caused the booms in the Bodie and Aurora Mining Districts, which were discovered at about the same time as Masonic. Sporadic mining was carried on by individuals and several companies were organized, but operations remained on a small scale until 1902.

The Pittsburg-Liberty Mine was opened that year and considerable activity ensued in the district. In 1907, the Pittsburg-Liberty Co. had a 10-stamp mill and cyanide plant. In 1909 the Chemung mine was discovered at some distance from the Pittsburg-Liberty works. Very rich ore was found in the Chemung and the property operated until about 1938. The Sierita mine and several other properties were opened at about the same time as the Chemung.

In Masonic Gulch were three settlements: Upper Town, Middle Town and Lower Town, about a half mile apart. Each had a boardinghouse or small hotel. In Middle Town was also a general merchandise store.

The lumber company delivered a considerable quantity of lumber to Masonic. It was hauled by six-horse teams from Bodie via the Geiger Grade road, a distance of 16 miles, passing over a 9200-foot summit. At 8000 feet, Masonic's elevation is a bit lower than that of Bodie.

Activity in the Masonic District slackened off a bit around 1910 or 1911, but the Chemung property continued to operate until about 1938. Since then, except for small prospecting, the district has been idle.

xiii. Oil in Mono Basin

Oil indications of various sorts were discovered from time to time in the Mono Basin and on the hills sloping toward the lake. During 1908-09 an oil well was drilled on Paoha, the larger of the two islands in Mono Lake. Lumber for the derrick was delivered from our lumber company to Warm Springs siding on the east shore, from where it was barged to the island. The well is reported to have reached a depth of 1500 feet when operations were abandoned. All that developed was a large flow of hot water.

Another well, to a depth of about 1200 feet, I believe, was drilled on Dechambeau ranch just north of Mono Lake; it too gave only hot water. A third well at the Carnonica ranch near the foot of Cottonwood Canyon, about nine miles, was reported a failure at a shallow depth. Perhaps with modern equipment capable of great depths, results might be different.

This oil derrick is on Paoha Island, Mono Lake.

Mines and workings on the hill east of Bodie as of 1922 can be seen in this panorama. From left to right: Cyanide plant; Bulwer tunnel; Hobart; Bechtel, near ridge; Standard, on ridge; Bulwer, considerably below it; Belvidere, just below that; Mono, at right edge of picture. The pano-

rama is concluded on the following pages. Below, the picture to the left is the brick mill of the Syndicate mine, built like a cathedral. Near the Bodie Tunnel mill, right below, seven Bodie boys enjoy a dip in the pond while friends watch from the bank. The picture dates from 1898.

Continuing the panorama of mine workings on the hill east of Bodie, left to right: Mono; Goodshaw; Oro, in the fold of the book; Red Cloud, over the ridge above the white Catholic church; Noonday, near the ridge; Spaulding and Snowdrift, below it at right; Blue Vein, far right. The Standard cyanide plant, below, made possible the recovery of gold from materials previously dumped as waste. At the bottom of the other page is an interior view of the cyanide plant.

The Red Cloud hoisting works was powdered with snow inside, when the 1922 picture above was made. The left-hand cage is at the floor level, while the one at the right is deep underground, with safety gate lowered. The hoist was operated by flat cable, which can also be seen reeled on the steam hoist in the 1951 picture at the top of the other page. The underground picture (in the Standard mine) shows a cage in one compartment of the shaft while the cage in the empty compartment was at the surface. This was called balanced hoisting, for the steam engine had only to cope with the load but did not have to use steam to handle the considerable weight of the cages and cables. Balance was achieved by what amounted to a gear ratio in the winding of the cables.

The mine shown above is the Red Cloud. After the first World War, most of the mine operations around Bodie were carried on by leasers such as those shown at the Bodie shaft, below.

The building with the flat roof in the above picture was built in 1918 by George Denham, Victor Cain and myself, as the first operation for the recovery of gold and silver from the mine dumps and surface ground of the old Standard property. In later years the operation was carried on by the Roseklip Co., whose plant was in the lighter building, above the dark structure formerly housing the railroad office, in the picture below.

For many years after the coming of the railroad, Chinamen found it profitable to bring piñon firewood to Bodie packed on burros, as in the upper picture, opposite. Around the corner from the Methodist Church was the home of Jim Cain, with its "greenhouse" window, left. At the bottom is shown the house where Theodore Hoover lived and where his famous brother Herbert sometimes visited. Jim Cain's Bodie Bank, with its ornate false front, is shown above, next to what was then the Post Office. Inside the bank, below, are Stuart Cain and Ed Stinson, surrounded by calendars dating from 1907 to 1913 and enough pin-up pictures to stock a miners' boarding house. (*above and two lower, opposite: Frasher's Fotos, Pomona, Calif.*)

THE BODIE BANK,

No. 390   M. J. Walsh   Bodie, Cal. Apr 16 187

has deposited in this B

Two Hundred   DOLLARS, Goes to

payable to the order of himself   on

return of this Certificate. Properly Endorsed

$200   W. H. Pope   Cash

CERTIFICATE OF DEPOSIT

THE BODIE BANK.

$50

★50★

The Bodie Bank

Bodie Cala Aug 3 1881

Pay to the order of B. Nathan & Co

Fifty   Dollars

The Bank of California   Geo H Winterburn

San Francisco, Cal.

No. 16716   CASH

The cashier's check, lower left, has been safeguarded, 1880-style, by having its value punched through the paper below the written amount. Payment of a two-cent federal tax on the document is indicated by the diamond-shaped background printing in the center. On these pages are three fine examples of Aurora brick construction. At the left, behind the buggy seating J. S. Cain, J. Woodbury, Alex McCone and Harry Gorham, is an iron-doored store building. Above is the entrance to the Post Office, with Jessie Bell in the doorway. Her brother Earl Bell is in the buggy with Dolly Cain. Below, Jim Cain, third from the right, stands before his residence in Aurora.

In the shadow of a stately brick building, a canvas-topped freight wagon drawn by 14 horses and mules stops on Aurora's Main Street. This had been built as a courthouse for Mono County, California, and served as such until an 1863 survey determined that Aurora was in Nevada. It then became the Esmeralda County courthouse, until Aurora became part of Mineral County. By 1907, when the above picture was taken, the building may have become a hotel or boarding house. A triangular dinner bell hangs from the corner of the balcony. By the Fourth of July in 1914 Aurora was in a new boom and the building had received fresh paint, a different balcony railing and a new lease on life as the Hotel Warren, which appears below, decorated for the holiday.

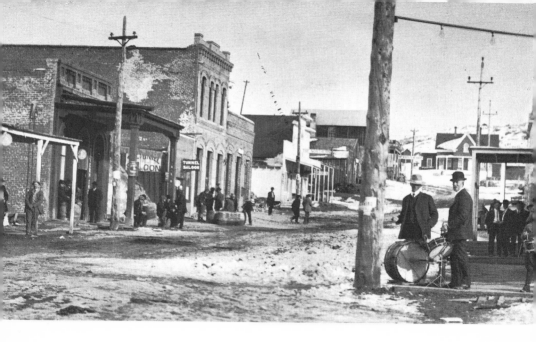

The wintry 1914 picture of Aurora, above, suggests some sort of celebration which brought out the drums in the right foreground. The life and activity evident in the upper picture are quite absent from the one below. Sagebrush lines the same street. John Peters waves from the running board of his Model T Ford, while my brother Gus leans against the fender and I stand there in my high top mining boots.

By the early 1900s Mark Twain had become so famous that the shack he is said to have lived in became an attraction for visitors to Aurora. Two carloads of tourists double-park in front of it, above. The cabin was later moved to Wingfield Park in Reno. Down the road can be seen the back of the ex-courthouse. The people in the picture below, standing before a store, can only be identified as residents of Aurora during its earlier boom years, perhaps in the 1880s.

The mill of the Cain Consolidated Mining Co. in Aurora appears above, while the mine and mill crews are shown in the interior photograph, below.

This panorama shows Aurora just about as it appeared when I first saw the place in 1908. The former courthouse was the biggest building in town. Jim Cain's house appears just to the right of the fold, facing away from the camera. The first big brick building on the near side of Main Street was the wreck of an old hospital when I was there; twenty years earlier it had been Angus McLeod's Exchange Hotel. Mark Twain's cabin

would be at the upper left, out of sight, just this side of the gabled brick house that looks down Main Street. Also associated with Mark Twain was the mine works that appear high on the hillside, just to the left of the fold; it was here that he became, as he wrote, "a millionaire overnight." Unfortunately for him, he promptly lost that million.

The Jesse Knight interests built the big 500-ton stamp mill near Aurora in 1912. The cottages and shops of the "dry" company town, Mangum, below, were built over the hill from Aurora at that time, as part of the town's last revival.

The Dunderberg was a mine at Castle Peak, south of Bridgeport. Ruins of its buildings are shown above. Below, at Rhinedollar Lake near the Tioga Pass road at the top of Lee Vining Creek, are Jim Cain, a power company clerk and myself. We are locating the Australian Copper Queen claim and have posted a notice, protected from the weather by the "Sunny Monday" box in front of me. (*Above, Frasher's Fotos, Pomona, Calif.*)

None of the mining camps had a more spectacular setting than Lundy at the head of Lundy Lake and at the foot of Mill Creek Canyon. The May Lundy mine perched precariously on the talus high above the town. Its mill, below, connected with the mountainside mine by means of an aerial tramway. Pulleys and other fittings for the cable can be seen at the top of the mill building.

The Consolidated Mining Co.'s mill, above, was located in the woods at High Grade, California. The big flywheel and some debris are all that now remain of the Mammoth Mining Co. mill in the Lake Mining District. It was already pretty much of a ruin when the picture below was taken.

The Pittsburg-Liberty works were in Masonic Gulch, east of Bridgeport. The mine headframe appears above. Below are the ten-stamp mill and cyanide plant.

AMUSEMENTS.

GOOD NEWS FOR THE BALD HEADS.

GENTLEMEN BE ON HAND

AT

MINERS' UNION HALL

FRIDAY, AUG. 6, 1880.

MILLE ALBISUERS'

Female Model Artist and Living Art Pictures.

POSITIVELY NO LADIES

Admitted under any consideration.

The handsomest formed woman on the earth.

SEEING THE ELEPHANT

In all its glory.

"High Life In Paris."

Reserved Seats at Phlegar & Harris'.

Opera glasses to rent for near sighted gentlemen at the Miners' Union Hall, on the night of performance.

Doors open at 7 o'clock ; Trouble commences at 8 o'clock ; Agony over at 10 o'clock P. M.

For particulars see large pictorial printing and small bills.

KEEP YOUR EYES ON THE DATE.

| Admission | - | - | - | - | - | $1 00 |
| Reserved Seats | - | - | - | - | $1 50 |

ju27td

ENTERTAINMENT!

FOR THE BENEFIT OF

JOHN HOLLAND,

A SUFFERER BY THE LATE EXplosion at the Bodie Mine, at

MINERS' UNION HALL,

SATURDAY, AUGUST 7TH, 1880.

Bulwer's great emotional play of

LADY OF LYONS,

OR

LOVE AND PRIDE,

Will be put on the boards by the

BEST TALENT OF BODIE

SEE SMALL BILLS.

Tickets $1.   Reserved Seats $1 50.   jv23

PICNIC GROUNDS

SIGOURNEY FLAT,

NEAR THE RICHER MINE.

ISAAC MISMORE, Prop.

HOTELS AND RESTAURANTS.

STEWART'S HOTEL,

Lower Main Street,

BODIE, - - - California.

Is under the direct supervision of Mrs. Stewart. The tables are supplied with the best the market affords. Lady attendants give every possible attention to patrons. Patronage solicited.
fe12-tf   MRS. M. Y. STEWART.

MINT CHOP STAND.

GOLD BRICK SALOON.

J. R. ABRAMS, Proprietor.

I WOULD INFORM MY FRIENDS and the Public that I have fitted up an elegant

CHOP STAND

AT THE

GOLD BRICK SALOON.

Dishes served to order at a moment's notice, prepared to suit the taste of patrons.
ju28tf

Bodie *Standard News*, August 3, 1880

CHAPTER FOUR

FUN AND PRANKS IN BODIE

i. *Latter-day "bad man"*

By the time I came to Bodie the population was in general a wholesome one and the "bad man" days were definitely over. Nevertheless, the tradition persisted and there were always some tough characters. I remember one fellow who was troublesome in this way. We might as well call him "Sam."

The Indians used to talk about him as a "squaw man"; maybe this is why he seemed to think he had to live up to the "bad man" image. At any rate, he did so pretty effectively when he was under the influence of liquor.

On one occasion he picked on a fellow whose name might have been "Frank." Since Sam was notoriously quick to draw his gun, Frank knew he could not handle him by direct physical attack. Nevertheless, he was determined to square matters with the obnoxious Sam.

Sam generally left his gun in his cabin during the day when he was working, so Frank sneaked in there and filed the firing pin off the hammer, then carefully replaced the gun just as it had been so Sam wouldn't suspect that anything had happened to it. Frank then hung a small steel bar from a leather thong through a hole in his right pocket so that it was concealed in his pants leg. His plan was to pick a fight to the extent that Sam would pull his gun. This would give Frank the excuse to hit him over the head with the steel bar and then claim self-defense.

Fortunately others intervened in time to prevent a possible killing.

Sam frequented circles and activities that brought him into conflict with the law, so that he was a familiar figure in the court, sometimes as a defendant, sometimes as a witness. Once he was called to testify in the defense of a Chinaman accused of selling whiskey to Indians. The trial was held in the back room of the McAlpine saloon. The Chinaman demanded and got a jury trial, although only five or six men could be found to serve on the jury.

Sam testified that he had never seen the Chinaman give any whiskey to the Indians. Shown a bottle about a third full of whiskey which had been offered in evidence, Sam admitted that he had seen the bottle before, but declared that as far as he knew, the Chinaman must have used the missing whiskey for making mince pies.

The case went to the jury which retired but soon sent word that it wanted the evidence, the bottle of whiskey. Presently the jury returned to the courtroom with the verdict of "not guilty" for want of sufficient evidence to determine if the bottle actually contained whiskey. The jurors had consumed the contents in the process of testing it.

On another occasion when Sam got himself well filled with whiskey, he and a like-minded friend, Dan, decided to shoot up the town. Sam mounted his cayuse, "Banjo" and rode up Main Street shooting his pistol at the hat Dan was tossing in the air. Opposite McAlpine's saloon Dan jumped on the horse behind Sam; they rode across the street and over the wooden sidewalk right into the saloon carrying the front door with them. Inside, they tried to shoot the glasses off the bar with the horse prancing and bucking all over the place. As the customers scrambled out of the way, the bartender tried to take a whack at the intruders with a poker from the stove. Finally with a leap, the horse cleared out of the saloon and Dan fell off.

The celebrants were locked up by the sheriff and brought before the justice of the peace. This official was at the time preparing to move out of Bodie with his family and did not want his departure delayed. It was his duty to try the case, of course, but he tried to handle it as quickly as possible. A plea of "not guilty" would have prolonged the proceedings, and word was passed Sam and Dan in their cells that a "guilty" plea might be to their advantage and result in a light sentence in the local jail. Accordingly when the case came up for trial, their plea was "guilty" and the judge promptly sentenced them to a long sojourn in the county jail at Bridgeport.

This judge had had trouble with these men before and probably decided that here was an opportunity to square matters a bit. At all events, he had the last laugh and promptly left town.

ii. An unhappy "corpse"

There was one old character who had developed a great liking for hard liquor and in his later years was "under the weather" quite a bit of the time. Once after a spree he was found lying in the sagebrush and some of the town's gentlemen decided to try to teach him a lesson and perhaps get him on the "water wagon."

From a dry goods store they obtained a large packing box and took it over to the drunk's resting place. As the box was too short to cover him, they knocked out one end and placed it over him with his feet sticking out.

When he started to move and mumble in the box, the group gathered around and conducted a funeral service. Some commented how sad they were at the passing of the deceased. They all ignored the fact that by now the victim was pounding on the box and shouting, "I ain't dead! I ain't dead!" The services concluded with dropping earth on the box and intoning, "Ashes to ashes, dust to dust . . ." Then the mourners departed and adjourned to a nearby store.

It was some time before the "deceased" came sufficiently to life to crawl out of the open end of the box. Excited and sobered, he came to the store wanting to know who was responsible. He was referred to a paper posted in the store window announcing his demise and the sale of his possessions at public auction the following day. He assured everyone that he was very much alive and that there would be no sale of his belongings. He remained on the "water wagon" for some time after this experience.

iii. Whimsical election

Mono County was never heavily populated. During the years of mining operations there were enough voters in Bodie alone to swing a county election. On at least one occasion this political power was used for a practical joke.

"Zeke Jones" might have been the name of a former county official who lived in Bodie and became something of a nuisance. After leaving public life he soured and rather lived the life of a cantankerous hermit. Some of the Bodie boys got together in a scheme which would at least be a good joke on "Jones" and which might get him painlessly out of town.

They held an informal meeting and decided to nominate him for another county office which would keep him in Bridgeport and away from Bodie. "Jones" was elated at the decision to nominate him. He felt greatly honored and entered earnestly into the campaign for election.

Many voters thought this was a joke and most were sure there was no chance of his being elected. Much to the surprise of the voters "Jones" made the grade and was installed in his new office in Bridgeport. The Bridgeporters did not appreciate this at all and Bodie had a good laugh at their expense.

While "Jones" was no great success in his new job, he did no harm in it either. He was not returned to office.

iv. Amusements

Of course there were saloons galore in Bodie. On the west side of Main Stret were the Mattos, McAlpine, Commercial, Temple, Sawdust Corner and Marks; on the east were the saloons of the Occidental and U. S. Hotels and the McKenzie Brewery.

There was a large Chinatown near the town jail. Gambling was wide open despite California laws against it, but the tables and wheels always happened to be out of operation when officers of the law visited Bodie. Poker and solo were the favorite card games.

Bonanza Street was also known as Virgin Alley, for here flourished the red light district. Some of its best-known denizens were Big Bonanza, Big Nell, Rosa May, and Bull Con Josie. Activities continued here until the latter days of the camp.

Masonic and Odd Fellows lodges were chartered in 1879 and remained active for many years until finally consolidated with their brother lodges in Bishop, Inyo County. The Masons thus left Bodie in December, 1918, The Odd Fellows a year later. The Masonic Hall was destroyed in the 1932 fire, but the Odd Fellows Hall was spared and survives as one of the few remaining buildings in town. Its upper floor was used for the lodge room and the lower for athletic activities.

The Miners' Union was organized in Bodie in December, 1877. Its headquarters Union Hall still stands and is now used as a museum. Here were countless entertainment and social events through the years, including memorable Christmas parties. A large decorated tree was placed on the stage and gifts were brought and placed under it for the children as well as for the adults. Santa Claus would call out the names for the distribution of the gifts, which were often on the humorous side for adults.

Some advertisements in the Bodie *Standard News* for August 3, 1880, tell of events which took place in the Miners Union Hall and suggest the type of entertainment available in Bodie during its boom years (see illustration, page 118).

v. *Holiday sports*

People would often entertain each other in their homes when I first came to Bodie. The roads were in such bad condition that there was little thought of going out of town, which always meant a long, tiresome buggy trip. As the automobile came to dominate transportation, social life at home declined and trips to such places as Reno, Carson City, Tonopah and other towns became hard to resist.

For sports, Bodie had a racetrack with a grandstand and a baseball field. Holiday doings there were something to behold, particularly during the summer months when outdoor activities were attractive. Decoration Day, Labor Day, and especially the

Fourth of July were always big occasions in town. The mines and the lumber company would shut down for a big three-day celebration which would begin on the third. To enliven the occasion there would be parades, races, tugs of war, drilling and shoveling contests and baseball games.

One Fourth of July baseball game, which pitted the married men against the single men, was notable for the keg of beer placed on first base. Anyone reaching the base was entitled to a glassful of the refreshing brew. Perhaps this was for the encouragement of the married men who otherwise might find it difficult to reach first.

These games and races provided plenty of opportunity for plain and fancy betting. One year the betting was particularly lively in anticipation of a race which would involve a six-foot college track star to whom I had given a summer vacation job at the request of the president of our company. Buell McCash could run 100 yards in ten seconds, and was studying to go into the ministry. He was a real competitor, eager for the races, and his running speed attracted so much respect that his vocational plans were overlooked. He trained for the coming race and aroused great interest and enthusiastic betting. Suddenly, on the eve of the race, he withdrew. He had heard about the purses for the winners and refused to race, because he did not want to hurt his amateur standing.

Our college student spent his summer at the mining camp with a determination to maintain standards of conduct and speech worthy of a man preparing for the ministry. I put him to work delivering lumber and wood in Bodie and in charge of two horses. "Mike" and "Madge" were large animals, but old and slow. It was a good show seeing Buell sitting high atop several cords of wood trying to get some action out of that team. His entreaties were made in such emphatic language as, "For goodness sake, Mike and Madge — get up!" Then he would shake the lines for emphasis.

All this was foreign language to those horses and for about a week they seemed to get slower and slower. Finally young McCash lost all patience and exploded. "You dirty sons of

bitches!" he yelled, emphasizing his words with a good applica-
tion of the whip. This brought the team into surprised action.
Matters moved along better after Buell learned to communi-
cate with his team by proper use of good old teamster talk.

The three-day holiday for the Fourth of July came always
at an awkward time for the finances of the men. Payday nor-
mally was on the tenth, for work performed during the previous
month. In July there were always many requests from employees for cash advances on their previous month's wages. One
year there was a shortage of cash available in town and I was
trying to figure out the best way to meet the situation when the
locomotive fireman, Slim Burke, came into the office.

I told him I was short of cash for the men and that he and
some of the others might have to cut down on their requests.
"How much do you need?" he asked and then added that he
might be able to help out. I thanked him for the offer, but felt
he would not have available the $500 or so that I needed.

Slim had been a sailor and turned prospector during the
winter months, returning each spring for several years to work
as a fireman on the locomotive. Generally he arrived with a
burro loaded down with his possessions. His scanty clothing
consisted of a pair of overalls and a matching denim jacket. He
also had a soft shirt to put on for dress occasions. To my surprise on this occasion he opened his jacket and took out $500
in currency from a money belt he had around his waist. In that
belt was more money he would have given me if necessary.

His general appearance seemed to belie any such prosperity
and I do not think anyone else was aware that he carried
money with him. Over the years that I knew him he was never
robbed, although he traveled in very isolated areas when
prospecting.

vi. Conviviality at Mono Mills

There was little in the way of entertainment for the men
working at Mono Mills, so they had to provide it for themselves. Gambling and drinking sometimes resulted in odd
situations.

When I first came the company operated a saloon in connection with the commissary there. It was not unusual to send out only part of the cash required for the payroll; the balance would always come over the bar on paydays. Naturally the liquor caused the usual fights, sometimes of a violent nature as there was no officer of the law to keep order. The liquor business was discontinued following a near-killing in 1908. After this, potables had to be smuggled into the camp by various means.

At one time the password for a bottle of bourbon was "turkey." One of the boys passing through the camp on his way to Bishop asked the clerk in the store if he could bring him anything on his return. The clerk promptly asked him to bring back a "turkey." After several days the man returned late at night. Next morning the clerk asked if he had remembered to bring the "turkey." The man said yes and that it was in the barn, which was considered a good hiding place. All primed for a goot shot of whiskey, the clerk opened the barn door. To his consternation a live bird flew out past him and into a tree from which it had to be shot down. It is not hard to imagine what the clerk had to say to the innocent messenger about that!

vii. The Chinese

The Chinese, as a rule, did not drink to excess, but there were exceptions. "Chan Yee," a cook employed in the Mono Mills boarding house, did more than his share of drinking and the practical jokers never overlooked opportunities to work on him when he was on a spree. It was Chan's custom to come to the commissary as soon as it opened in the morning and get a stiff drink of whiskey. Unless this was forthcoming there would be no breakfast.

One morning the cook came in as usual and the clerk poured out a large drink in a water glass. Chan promptly downed it in one gulp and as promptly erupted in a wild reaction, punctuated with colorful Chinese cussing. The supposed whiskey had turned out to be vinegar. There was no breakfast that morning.

Another time, when Chan was on a spree, he came to rest on the wooden floor of the blacksmith shop where he was found during the night. This was too good an opportunity for the jokers to miss and a couple of them went down to the shop and loosened the Chinaman's queue, stretching it along the floor and driving several staples over it close to his head.

When he awakened, the cook tried to get up but could not raise his head. He let out loud cries for help, and it took quite a time to quiet him before it was safe to remove the staples that held his "pigtail." Chan threatened to kill those responsible, and no doubt would have done so if he could have found out who they were. Needless to say, this was another morning without breakfast.

One summer during logging operations the boarding house in the camp had another Chinese cook whose name was Tim. He had to feed quite a crew of loggers, teamsters and others, as well as twenty or more horses and mules, for which hay and grain had to be provided.

Tim got along fairly well for a time, but presently complaints reached Tom Miller at the Mills store that the crew was good and tired of being fed stew all the time. Investigation revealed that steaks, roasts and a variety of meats had been sent to the boarding house. It also revealed that Tim was feeding himself in style and disposing of meat to his Indian friends.

This left him short on the better cuts of meat, so he kept supplementing the supply by trapping chipmunks, of which there were plenty around the stable, and adding them to the stew. I had to fire Tim and get him out of the logging camp in a hurry, for the crew was ready to give him a good beating for serving them chipmunks.

Ah Yang was a funny little Chinaman with a squeaky voice, who peddled vegetables, chickens and other eatables in Bodie and sometimes in Aurora, where he lived in a small cabin. Like most Chinese he loved to gamble and poker was his forte. Sometimes he was an easy mark for his gaming companions.

Once in a saloon in Aurora he could not figure out why he was such a consistent loser. When he had a good hand several of the other players would drop out. Finally he solved the mystery, or was tipped off. When he was playing he was always seated with his back to the wall of the saloon, where there was a large mirror. Ah Yang had a bad habit of exposing his cards in such a way that the players sitting opposite him could see them in the mirror behind him. Ah Yang's loud complaints were to no avail, but from then on he always took care to have a different seat at the poker table.

viii. The Indians

Many of the Paiute Indians were employed by the railroad company and a large colony of them lived at Mono Mills in the summer. The encampment consisted of wickiups, shacks made from old lumber and whatnot. Some of their names were unusual for Indians and others were just unusual: Pat Gregory, Young Charlie, Doby Jim, Two Bits and Lefty Jack, just to mention a few.

When Lefty Jack was working at the logging camp one summer, he and his squaw and their young son, a couple of years old, were living at the camp. Some of the men working there asked Jack what the boy's name was. Jack said he had no name and the crew at the camp thought that this matter should be attended to promptly.

While most of the crew were in high liquid spirits after their supper one evening, they discussed the problem of naming Jack's young son. Several names were suggested, but they were all discarded. Finally one of the boys suggested Jasper. This happened to be the first name of the logging camp foreman, and it was immediately and enthusiastically approved. A delegation of the men thereupon waited on Jack and his squaw to inform them of the decision that henceforth the boy's name would be Jasper Jack. This name was entirely agreeable to the father and mother.

The next day, news of the naming of the boy reached the foreman and his wife. He had not been present at the caucus, and had not been consulted at all on the matter. The air, of course, was blue and the crewmen ran for cover. No amount of invective or argument could change the name; the boy grew to manhood and still goes by the name of "Jasper Jack."

In the fall and during the winter months, the Indians who worked at Mono Mills would move to various places in Mono Basin. A couple of families moved to the area near Warm Springs on the east shore of Mono Lake. There, during the duck season, they shot many ducks for themselves and for sale. Ducks were plentiful and the east shore of the lake was an excellent place for hunting, as very few people except railroad employees ever visited the area.

The Indian named Jack had a large-caliber, long-barrel shotgun. A regular shell in this gun was not enough for him and he loaded small scraps of metal for added destructiveness. For hours he would wait in the sand dunes close to the lake, hoping for a pot shot at the ducks.

Loaded with a shotgun shell and all that scrap metal, the gun's recoil was so strong that Jack could not hold it, so he placed it on the ground, carefully aimed at the spot where the ducks would congregate. Well shielded from sight in the sand and sagebrush, Jack would wait until the ducks were grouped together; then he would lie on the ground and pull the trigger. The result was a slaughter of ducks and as soon as he had fired he was on his feet, a club in his hand, rushing into the lake. Waist-deep, he would whale away at the birds that were wounded and struggling to get out of reach. It was a sight to behold, but the effort was evidently worthwhile, for it was not unusual for Jack to bag from ten to twenty ducks from the one shot and his club.

Indians were often involved in funny situations, particularly where the United States Post Office was concerned. There was, for instance, the Indian who came into the Bodie Post Office and asked if the postmaster had any stamps. Informed that many were available, the Indian asked, "How many you got?" The postmaster said there were several hundred, then asked how many he wanted. The Indian pondered the information for a moment, then replied, "One."

Another Indian came into the Post Office to ask if there was any mail for him. The postmaster knew this man as well as any member of his own family, but, for the life of him, he could not think of the Indian's name. He fumbled with the mail for a moment in embarrassment, finally gave up and asked what the name was. The Indian thought this over for a moment and replied, "The same as it was yesterday." No wiser as to the man's identity the postmaster told him there was no mail for him and to come again tomorrow.

Once when Mark Kerr and I were about to leave Mono Mills by train for Bodie, we saw an Indian squaw with a young papoose on her back. Mr. Kerr wanted a picture of the mother and child and got out a medium-sized box camera. He took a snapshot, we got on the train to Bodie and thought no more of the incident.

A week or so later, when I was on a trip to the Mills, a clerk in the store told me that the Indians were excited and had demanded to know what had been in the black box. The baby had died and they thought the box had something to do with it.

We spoke to the Indians and tried to explain that the box only took pictures. They asked to see the picture, but Mr. Kerr had returned to Tonopah and I had no copy of it at the time. I promised to send for one at once. When the picture arrived I gave it to the Indians and explained how it was taken with the camera. I was finally able to convince them that it had no connection with the child's illness and death.

The Indians loved to gamble. For one of them to lose all his money, saddles and horses at one sitting was not unusual. Then too, as everywhere else, the Indians at Mono Mills loved firewater when they could get it.

A certain old Indian who often caused trouble once managed to get some firewater in the form of wood alcohol on a trip to Bodie. He returned to Mono Mills where a party was soon in full swing. Two of the Indians died from the effects of this wrong kind of alcohol, but the old buck, who had probably taken more than the others, managed to pull through.

One of the Indians, a good worker, would get drunk at the first chance; when alcohol was unavailable he would go in for dope or hop from a Chinaman in Bodie. When he had a craving, there was no stopping him from going to Bodie. If there was no train at the time, he would walk all the way to town from the Mills, over thirty miles along the track. He ran into trouble with the law several times. Early one morning, on the way to the Bodie town jail, this Indian broke away from the constable and ran up the hill toward the lumber yard with the officer in pursuit. He was outdistancing the constable, who fired a shot at him; the Indian only thought this called for more speed. His shoes must have bothered him, for he deliberately sat down and removed them, putting them under his arm, and away he went through the brush on his bare feet. The constable sent a few more shots to speed him on his way.

ix. Robbery

We had a small robbery in 1915. Early one morning Charlie Cease, the clerk in the store at Mono Mills, phoned to tell me someone had broken into the so-called safe during the night and stolen about $100 in company funds.

Untouched in the safe were envelopes containing funds left by the men for safekeeping, with the understanding that the company would not be responsible for any loss. This suggested that the job may have been pulled by someone employed in the camp who felt that if the men's money was not taken, they would not be too interested in finding the thief.

I asked Charlie not to mention the theft, but to look around behind the store near the door for footprints and other possible clues. While the clerk was doing this, "Fat" McLaughlin, the boarding house cook, came to the store for breakfast supplies. Of course he asked what Charlie was looking for.

The clerk did not want to say what had occurred and casually mentioned that someone passing through had dropped a twenty-dollar gold piece — then in common use — and could not find it. Right away "Fat" was more interested in this bit of news than in preparing breakfast.

As soon as he could get away from the kitchen he set up a screen such as is used in mixing mortar, and started to shovel the sand against it to sift out that gold piece. The day grew hot and shoveling the mixture of volcanic pumice and sand was hard work. The immense cook was not in very good spirits at not finding the coin. By now Charlie was afraid to tell "Fat" the truth, fearing a bad beating.

None of us who knew the facts disclosed them to the cook and the thief got away with the spoils.

For all of Bodie's vaunted lawlessness, the Bodie Bank was robbed only once during its entire existence. This was in September, 1916, long after the lusty boom years of Bodie's rollicking and riproaring youth.

No dashing, desperate gunman burst into the place; nobody terrorized the customers and staff; nobody rode wildly and triumphantly down Main Street, shooting and shouting, clutching a fortune in loot. On the contrary, the job was done by burglars who broke into the bank at night. They didn't do too badly, though, for they made away with about $2,000 in cash, some bullion, and valuables stored in strong boxes in the vault which belonged to individuals and various of the unions.

x.   Senseless killing

A drunken orgy and its senseless aftermath in November, 1915, aroused and saddened all of Mono County. Two Mexican laborers went on a rampage in Mono Basin, broke into a store at Mono Lake, stole guns and ammunition and then set out to raid some of the ranches. They frightened women and children and at one place set fire to a large haystack.

When the news reached Sheriff James P. Dolan in Bridgeport, he set out for Mono Lake, accompanied by a driver. At the lake he learned that the Mexicans were last seen going south on the road along the west shore. The sheriff and a companion drove a short distance, presently noticing the Mexicans in the brush beside the road. He drove past them and then got out of the buggy and walked back toward the Mexicans. He had no fear nor thought of gun play and was confident he could take the men into custody without trouble. Without warning, the Mexicans shot Sheriff Dolan and fled from the scene.

The needless killing aroused everyone in the county and posses were formed to hunt down the Mexicans and avenge the sheriff's murder. It took some doing, as the Mexicans cleverly made their way on foot along creeks to cover their trail. They were reported seen at different places from time to time. Indians finally picked up their tracks which led across the flat south of Mono Lake into the timber near Mono Craters. Finally a mounted posse found them entrenched behind some fallen trees.

There was no question of surrender. One of the opening shots by the Mexicans sent a bullet through the hip pocket of one of the horsemen, puncturing a can of tobacco. Quickly the posse dismounted. After considerable gun fire and some very close calls, one of the Mexicans aiming over a log was hit in the head. The other was also promptly dispatched.

It was considered a miracle that there were no casualties in the posse, as the Mexicans were known to be good shots.

xi. A windy funeral

Sometimes a sad occasion produces a humorous situation. This was the case during a funeral in Bodie. Remains of the deceased had been prepared by undertaker Bill Owens, an ex-miner. After the ceremony the casket was loaded on a delivery wagon which had a high seat overlooking the team of horses. The driver was waiting for the undertaker to climb up beside him for the trip to the cemetery. Meanwhile the mourners were forming a procession behind the improvised hearse for the sad trip to the cemetery.

Despite a brisk wind which blew down from the Sierra, raising swirls of dust from Bodie's main street, Bill maintained all the dignity of his profession. As befitted the solemn occasion, he was garbed in a black frock coat which extended to his knees. Unfortunately, both solemnity and dignity were shattered and replaced by merriment and guffaws from the assembled mourners as a gust of wind blew the tails of his coat over his head, disclosing a large patch of white underwear where the seat of his pants was missing.

xii. A man's best friend

Freid Walker was known about Bodie as a sturdy, hard-working man of many accomplishments, one who could be depended upon. He was also known for his constant companion of many years, the dog he called "Blue." This dog was about the size of a setter, had albino eyes and hair of an unusual bluish shade which accounted for his name.

One day I had occasion to look up Freid to ask him to do some work for us. At the time he was occupying a room on the second floor of the "Hydro" building at the corner of Green and Main Streets, Bodie. I climbed the stairs to his room and found him just getting up, sitting on the edge of his bed. Blue was not with him, and after arranging with Walker about the work, I asked him what had become of his pet, saying that I missed seeing the animal.

"Oh, Blue is right here," said Walker pointing to the rug on which his feet were resting. Sure enough, he had made a rug out of the pelt after the animal died, so as to have his beloved dog with him always.

Mono County's graceful courthouse in Bridgeport was the scene of a Fourth of July celebration in the mid-1920s, above. Looking west toward the distant Sierra Nevada, the courthouse dome rises above the garage to the right of Bridgeport's Main Street. In the foreground is a sedan bearing, on its spare tire cover, the trade-mark of photographer Frasher whose fine work makes it possible for present generations to know what the land east of the Sierra was like in that other age, before fast highways made it easily accessible. On the opposite page is Bodie's jail, still standing — empty — at the northern edge of town west of Main Street. *(Opposite and below: Frasher's Fotos, Pomona, Calif.)*

Next to the Odd Fellows' hall, above, was one of Bodie's few brick buildings, a lodging house belonging to the Dechambeau family. In Bodie's
ghost town days it became a saloon. The two structures still huddle
together at the southern end of Main Street. Below, a convivial group
lines up for a picture in front of a popular saloon, "The Commercial, J.
McAlpine, Prop." On the other page are inside and outside views of
Bodie's finest hall, which now serves as a museum. The trees in the lower
view were cut and brought to Bodie as a customary part of holiday deco-
rations. (*Opposite above: Frasher's Fotos, Pomona, Calif.*)

Bodie's baseball team had natty uniforms just as any major or minor league club. Apparently Bodie's chill wind was blowing during the game shown below, for the spectators seem to prefer standing in the sunshine rather than sitting in the shade on the grandstand at the race track where games were played. The little girls in white on the decorated wagon, opposite, carry pennants inscribed with the names of the states. Even the MONO engine was decorated in the spirit of the glorious Fourth.

Bodie's Miners' Union, dressed up in holiday best for the Labor Day parade, stops with its band for a picture just before reaching the union hall on Main Street. Part of the traditional holiday festivities in Bodie, as in Tonopah, were the contests of mining skills: mucking, opposite above, and below it, drilling. The donkey doesn't seem to mind the juvenile load, but the lad at the tail end seems worried about sliding off.

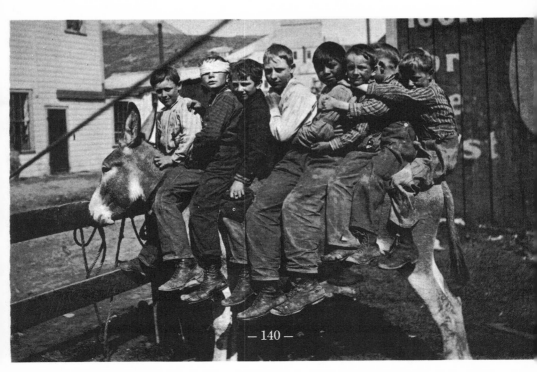

Chinatown was on King Street which appears in the 1911 picture, below. A number of its residents appear in these pages. The queued gentleman above is identified as Quong Yee, merchant. The man with the apron is Charlie, who is pictured by the Cain house where in 1916 he was cook. At the far right is the scholarly-appearing Quong Ying Lung.

The engrossed Indians above are playing the "hand game" at Hammond's store, Mono Lake. On the porch of the Mono Mills store, below, is Lefty Jack conferring with the putteed Dave Speed, our manager, The well-fed Indian on horseback seems to have had plenty of pine nuts; I don't think that was his own horse. Four squaws, a black dog and an Indian man stand behind Bodie's Odd Fellows' Hall.

The Indian sitting by the improvised shelter on Bodie Hill, above, was named Quesso. The Paiute "residence," below, is made from tules; the shallow basket was used to net fish and Mono Lake shrimp.

The Paiute squaw, above, is standing by Jim Cain's brick home in Aurora.
The one in the dugout canoe, below, displays samples of her handiwork.

CHAPTER FIVE

FACILITIES AND WEATHER

i. Buildings and facilities

Nearly all the buildings in Bodie were of frame construction. The stores and better residences were substantial as compared with the many board-and-batten shacks. A couple of the buildings were built of brick and behind stores were cellars of rock construction with thick walls and floors for storage of canned goods and other valuable merchandise.

In such a town fire protection is vital and Bodie made provision for it. There was a reservoir on the hill with pipelines leading to hydrants spotted about the town. The Volunteer Fire Department was organized and equipped with hand-drawn hose carts. The equipment should have been ample to handle almost any fire, but in both of Bodie's big conflagrations troubles developed which seriously hampered fire-fighting. The screens in the reservoir were clogged, for one thing, and the volunteers failed to understand the function of left-handed British hydrants which were wrenched and jammed shut instead of open.

The main domestic water supply was, and still is, piped in from Rough Creek Springs, about four miles west of town, at an elevation of over 9000 feet. This supply was supplemented by other springs nearer to town. The quality of the water was a matter of pride to the people of Bodie.

Horse-drawn stages connected Bodie with Hawthorne, Bridgeport, Mono Lake and Lundy. Telephone lines went to these and other nearby communities. The pioneering electric system will be described at length later in this chapter.

Bodie had a school, two churches, five breweries, a soft drink bottling works, a foundry, an assay office and large stables and shops to serve the heavy teaming. On Main Street were the U.S. and Occidental Hotels, several general merchandise stores, an assortment of saloons, a doctor, a drug store and many other enterprises. There were also a Land Office, a Post Office, the Wells Fargo agency and the J. S. Cain-Bodie Bank.

ii. Hotel meals

Board and room in the hotels was at the rate of $35 a month with three meals a day. Restaurant meals in those days were in great contrast with the high priced service we know today. It was not unusual to have steaks, eggs and hot cakes for breakfast, all together if desired. On all tables were large dishes filled with canned fruit and trays holding big three-layer cakes to which you helped yourself. Almost everything served was made on the premises and prices were reasonable. A dollar would buy a big meal.

When I was living on the hill, I often came down to town for meals in the large dining room of the Occidental Hotel. One morning I was joined there by Dr. Dupuich, Bodie's resident physician at the time.

When we were trying to decide on our order for breakfast, big Warren Loose, one of the owners of the New Bodie Mining Co. syndicate, came in and sat at a table some distance from ours. He had a bag which he gave the waitress when she came for his order. He told her that the bag contained a dozen fresh eggs he had just bought at the Burkham store and he wanted them all soft boiled. Being a large man with a hearty appetite, he also ordered a stack of hot cakes and plenty of coffee.

When the waitress came for our order she suggested soft boiled eggs for us. The doctor and I hesitated, for we knew the great scarcity of fresh eggs in Bodie and hesitated to take our chances on the cold storage eggs usually served in restaurants. On the waitress' assurances that we would enjoy them this time, we decided to try our luck.

She brought us two eggs apiece and we noticed that each was marked with a cross in indelible pencil. We drew her attention to the marks and she explained that these were a part of the eggs Loose had brought in and that it was quite all right, for she also had an indelible pencil which she had used on cold storage eggs to replace these in his order. With the eight fresh eggs which he still had and the four storage ones he was none the wiser when he mixed the whole batch in a bowl. You never know what you are going to get!

iii Transport

Isolated as it was by miles of rugged mountain and desert terrain, Bodie had to depend on difficult and expensive means of moving goods and people between the camp and the more populous parts of the land. The Bodie & Benton railroad went only to Mono Mills. The nearest railroad connecting with the outside world was nearly fifty miles away, at Thorne, near Hawthorne, Nevada, by a primitive mountain road. This was the arduous route by which most people and goods came to Bodie.

When I first arrived on the horse-drawn stage, freight was hauled by big jerk-line teams like those I had seen at Tonopah. From the Thorne station of the Southern Pacific's narrow gauge Carson & Colorado, the cost was from $18 to $20 a ton to haul freight this way. Similar freight from Minden on the standard gauge Virginia & Truckee cost about $25 a ton.

Wells Fargo express rates into Bodie were very high, five to six dollars per pound on fruit, which came at a special rate. The rate on bullion was $7.50 on $1000 and up according to the grade of the bullion. The rate on gold coin was $5.50 per $1000. Wells Fargo service to Bodie was discontinued in 1912.

Parcel Post service was inaugurated in 1913. This allowed shipment by mail of fifty pounds per package and we were quick to seize the opportunity to ship most of our freight by this much cheaper means. We could make a substantial saving in shipping supplies to the company store at Mono Mills by parcel post, rather than the combined railroad and team freight charges.

— 151 —

Since the shipments were limited to fifty pounds and confined to the first and second parcel post zones, we arranged with shippers and wholesalers to send most of the groceries and even blacksmith coal from Sacramento and Reno, which were within the required zones. Canned goods and similar merchandise were repacked by the shippers to come within the weight and dimension limits set by the regulations. Sugar, stock salt, grain and coal were sacked in double bags to avoid damage from breakage.

Nearly all the merchants used parcel post and there resulted a terrible jam of goods at Thorne station, where trains were detained for long periods to unload parcel post for Bodie, Mono Lake and other points east of the Sierra. The stage line with the mail contract from Thorne to Bodie was swamped handling the shipments and had to add a dozen or more horses and extra wagons to handle the loads. At that time trucks were just coming into use here and a couple of them were also added for the hauling.

Complaints from people handling the extra freight led the Post Office to increase payments to the mail contractors to compensate for the extra expenses incurred. This increase in parcel post use had not been expected and new regulations limited shipments to 500 pounds per day. Shippers got around this by making successive 500-pound daily shipments until an order was filled, even on items such as sugar and grain which were customarily handled in lots of a ton or more.

iv. Electric power

When I came to Bodie in 1908 electric power was used to operate the mines and, to some extent, for illumination in the town. The power system belonged to the Standard Mining Co. and was primarily for its own operations, but some power was sold to businesses in the camp. Very few of the houses had electrical service.

Fifteen years before I came, this electric system was the talk of the mining world, for it was a pioneer in what was then considered long-distance transmission of power. Engineers came from around the world to observe the system and to apply its ideas to countless other installations.

It was the high cost of fuel which led the mining company to undertake the construction of this power system in 1892. Thomas H. Leggett, president and general manager, took Jim Cain and an engineer on a trip to measure the water in Green Creek about 13 miles from Bodie. The creek was dammed to form a reservoir, which they called the Dynamo Pond. From there a pressure pipe carried water to the generator in the power plant. A two-wire transmission line was built in a straight line from the Dynamo to the Standard works in Bodie. In those days it was believed that any deviation from a perfectly straight line would interfere with the transmission of power. There is said to have been some fudging of the distance in that 13-mile line, for the Stanley Electric Co., which furnished the equipment would not guarantee the operation in excess of 12 miles. Electric power had never before been transmitted over such a long distance.

The transmission line was completed in November, 1892; a month later the plant was completed and ready to run. Unfortunately for the company, which had shut down the mill to prepare for the change to electric power, the electrical apparatus did not reach Bodie until April, 1893, six months after it had been ordered. Numerous troubles and accidents had to be overcome and it was fully ten months after the plant should have been in action before it was able to use the electric power.

As delay followed delay many people in Bodie became skeptical about this newfangled contraption. The delay was costly to the mining company: dividends did not come to the stockholders; men on payrolls were laid off. Some people began to fear that the system would never work. Jim Cain was invited into the mill to observe the start of electrical operations. When the mill machinery began to operate, relief, pleasure and elation swept the camp. Bodie's electric system was now producing power and soon it attracted attention around the globe.

The mill and the mine were the first users of the power, but as the years went on, electricity was put to more and more use in Bodie. The capacity of the original Dynamo soon proved inadequate to meet the demand and a new generating plant was installed at Green Creek. A Pelton water wheel produced 350 horsepower to deliver 6600-volt, three-phase alternating current to the new three-wire transmission line which replaced the old two-wire direct current system.

This was the system which supplied the mines, mills and some places of business in Bodie when I arrived in 1908. Coal oil and gasoline lamps, lanterns and candles remained much in use in the homes and places of business.

v. A shocking prank

The Standard Mining Co. sent a construction foreman whom we might call "Bill" with a crew of several men to make repairs on the Green Creek power plant and the dam above it. During the work a couple of the boys thought of a joke to play on the others.

They drove nails around the seat of the outdoor "library" and connected them with wires from the lighting circuit. They were sure the results would be spectacular if the power happened to be turned on when the "library" was occupied. Unfortunately for them, the victim of their installation turned out to be none other than their foreman.

Bill was a big man who always wore a derby hat while working in the plant or mine, as it warned him to protect his head in low places. He entered the "library" and got ready to make himself comfortable for a few leisurely minutes with the Montgomery Ward catalog. He seated himself and immediately bounced up with a roar, hit the ceiling and crushed his hat down over his eyes. His exit from the place was fast and furious indeed.

For all his threats, he could not learn who the culprits were. As a result, the crew was not spared to complete the work and returned to Bodie in short order.

vi. Severe winters

Bodie's winters were severely cold. The thermometer would remain below zero, sometimes going as low as thirty below, for days at a time. This called for lots of heating, day and night, where people were. The cooking stoves were kept going as well as other heating stoves, most of which were made of sheet iron. They gave red-hot heat, but needed a lot of attention as they were hard to regulate for steady heat. Nearly everyone had a good supply of stove wood stored in the sheds for the winter.

Exposed water pipes often froze and broke unless they were well insulated. Toilets were of the outdoor type and those having them under cover adjoining a woodshed were indeed fortunate. Even then it meant bundling up for a trip to the shed on account of the cold. Those unfortunate souls who had to make the trip through the snow for some distance from the house usually wore overshoes and a heavy coat. It was no place to linger.

vii.   Uncomfortable sleigh ride

During a winter of heavy snowfall I made a trip to Hammond's (now Tioga Lodge, Mono Lake) from Bodie. From the Cain stables I hired a team of horses and a sleigh with a seat in front for two people and the gooseneck type of sled runners that extended well up in front of the sleigh.

Although the road had been broken through the snow after the storm, the going was slow on the uneventful twenty-mile trip. Mill Creek was spread out for a considerable distance, but frozen over so the team and sleigh crossed it easily.

At Hammond's I met Nat Smith, our caretaker from Mono Mills, who had skied over to meet me. After feeding and resting the team and ourselves, we started back for Bodie. It was a clear, cold moonlight night, but we were comfortable in our heavy clothing and blankets.

All went well until we reached Mill Creek. We were careful and the horses picked their way gingerly over the frozen stream, but when we were almost safely across, the team broke through the ice. The horses started plunging to get clear and the sleigh also broke through, letting in the ice and water. We found that we had lost the right-hand sled runner from the first knee all the way to the rear of the sleigh so that it tipped over and backward and we could not proceed on an even keel.

It was then impossible to repair the damage and it first looked as though we would have to ride the horses 15 miles to Bodie. This did not appeal to us and, after some experimentation, we found we could use the sleigh if we both leaned far over the curved dashboard and kept all the weight on the left side. This meant kneeling all the way to town. Fortunately we had a clear night and, after many stops to stretch cramped legs, we reached Bodie in the early morning.

As my comrade said, "We have kneeled enough tonight to make up for all the past years."

viii. High-proof warmup

During the winter months, when the railroad was shut down, it was still necessary to send supplies to Mono Mills, particularly when logs and wood were being cut. The trip generally took two days with a team of horses, from Bodie by way of the Goat Ranch and along the west side of Mono Lake to Rush Creek. From that point the snow got deeper toward the Mills, at their elevation about a thousand feet higher than the lake.

For the last six or seven miles it was usually necessary to attach snowshoes to the horses. These were made of steel plates about ten inches square, fitted with a clamp over the horse's hoof, with slots in the plate to engage the calks of the regular horseshoe and prevent the snowshoe from slipping off.

On one of these winter trips we carried a small keg of whiskey extract with the supplies for the timber contractors. The merchant did not explain to me that this extremely high-proof whiskey had to be diluted with water to cut it to a reasonable proof.

Hearing of my arrival with the supplies, the two contractors and four of their men came to the Mills on skis the following morning to pack the goods to their camp four miles farther on in the timber. We all decided to pitch in and try to break a road through the snow with the four horses available. It was hard, slow work, for the snow was at least four feet deep on the level and had many higher drifts.

After several hours of this work the men decided it was time for the lunch we had brought along. The contractors suggested that we all have a drink of whiskey and punched a hole in the keg. Since there were no cups or glasses, we broke open a case of canned tomatoes and took out several cans, cast the contents aside and used the cans for the libation.

After a couple of drinks of the stuff nobody was in any condition to continue work. It was something to see half a dozen men on skis staggering and falling over one another in the snow. We had gone only a mile from the Mills when we had to turn back to await another day.

ix. The new power system

In January 1911 a new and modern hydroelectric system went into operation, serving not only Bodie but also surrounding communities as far away as Aurora, Hawthorne and Fairview. The Pacific Power Co., which later became part of the California Electric Co., put up a power plant at Jordan in the Mono Lake Basin, below Lundy Lake.

The plant, equipment and employees were housed in modern concrete structures at the foot of Copper Mountain near the spot where an old smelter had stood for years.

For the first time electric power was available to the whole community of Bodie. The Green Creek power plant, which belonged to the Standard Mining Co., continued to serve company properties until 1923 when it was purchased by the Mono Mining Co. and moved to Sweetwater.

Meanwhile, the people kept their frame buildings tightly sealed against the rigors of the mountain winter which this year, as always, was severe with high winds, heavy snows and thermometer readings of twenty and more below zero. It was not unusual for roads to be closed for days at a time. Sometimes there would be a week or more when stages could not get into or out of Bodie.

In March 1911 the winter weather was particularly bad. A storm began on the sixth and continued unabated until the eighth. At the time I was living with my brother Gus, Nat Smith and Ed Stinson on the hill near the railroad and lumber company office. All water had to be packed to the house from a reservoir and the horses we kept in a nearby barn had to be led to the reservoir for water. This was difficult during a storm.

On the second day of this storm we decided to go to town until it was over, stopping at the Occidental Hotel on Main Street and leaving the horses in the Burkham barn nearby. We left the hill at eleven in the morning and did not reach Main Street, half a mile away, until nearly three in the afternoon. The snow was as high as the roofs of the houses and visibility was cut to a minimum. It took another hour to get the horses to the barn a couple of blocks down Main Street.

Suddenly that evening electric service in Bodie went dead. We assumed that a break had occurred in the transmission line and got out the old oil lamps that had served so well through the years. The storm let up the next day and efforts began on the monumental task of digging out and opening roads about town and to the outside world. We worked until dark clearing necessary local roads and paths and the night seemed very dark indeed, with the electricity still off. We figured it might be several days before repair crews could fix the broken places on the power lines. Telephone communication was also disrupted by the storm and it was not until the next morning that we had our first word from outside. It came by way of the line from Mono Mills, where the caretaker had been trying for 17 hours to make a connection with Bodie.

Meanwhile, at Hammond's Station, the people had been threatened during the storm by possible slides. The little hamlet stood on the edge of Mono Lake with high mountains rising immediately behind it. The safest place there was Hammond's store, which was built beneath a bluff which would cause a slide to split and go around the building

When the storm subsided, Jack Hammond organized a search party to determine what damage might have been done in the vicinity and to seek out any stranded people. Visibility was very poor, for the whole Mono Basin was covered with a heavy cold fog, "pokonip" as the Indians call it. The party could see no sign of the powerhouse at Jordan or its surrounding concrete buildings. West of the plant there was evidence of a big snowslide on the steep slope of Copper Mountain. This was unprecedented, for the powerhouse had been built on the site of an early-day smelter that had never suffered a slide. Apparently this one had wrecked the plant, but because of the fog the party could not determine the full extent of the damage.

Jack Hammond then sent a couple of men from his place to the Farrington Ranch where the nearest telephone was available. To skirt the snow-blocked road along the shore they had to row across Mono Lake to get there. The only telephone line open was to Mono Mills. Hammond's men were able to talk with the caretaker there by 3 p.m. It took him all night to reach the operator at Bodie and it was not until 8 a.m. the day after the storm let up that he was finally able to tell Jim Cain that the power plant had been wrecked.

We now knew why the lights were out, but did not know the fate of the people who worked at the plant. A rescue party with Bodie's physician was sent across the snow to the scene of the disaster. Dr. Krebs was not accustomed to using skis in cross-country travel and had to be helped along by a couple of good men. We called skis snowshoes those days and they were mostly homemade, with a single toe strap to hold them to the boots and a cleat to fit against the heel.

At the same time, a large party of men attacked the job of clearing the road out of Bodie. It was a terrible task breaking through that snow which lay in many places as deep as ten feet. The mines shut down and sent their men to help on the road, and other able men also joined in. Altogether there were about seventy men and ten horses on the job. That night we reached the summit toward Mono Lake, about two miles from town. The next day the same crew made about a mile and a half more, but that afternoon another storm began to fill the newly cleared road with snow borne by the heavy winds. Some of the men were along in years and not accustomed to such strenuous outdoor work. Snow froze on their faces and their clothes were like ice. The horses had trouble keeping on their feet and finally had to be unhitched from the light sleighs. The crew had to pull the sleighs to the top of the hill on the way back to town. Other horses, unencumbered by the sleighs, were driven ahead to break a track. Many of the men became snowblind and their faces were frostbitten, swollen and cracked. All were exhausted by the time they returned to town for a second night without electricity. It would take a week to clear the roads at this rate.

It took the rescue party some time to locate the powerhouse and surrounding buildings, for ten to twenty feet of snow covered the wreckage. Nothing was to be seen except the expanse of snow. The men probed through it with rods and finally started shoveling out trenches. At one place when they made a hole, a cat jumped out, scampered off and disappeared over the snow never to be seen again.

It turned out that all the buildings had collapsed under the pressure of the avalanche. The rescue crew's task proved grim in the extreme, as body after crushed body was found in the wreckage of the concrete cottages. At one place they heard a scream which caused them to redouble their efforts. They found Mrs. Agnes Mason, wife of one of the operators, alive but pinned in her bed beside her dead husband. Their cottage had collapsed, but one of the concrete wall slabs had caught on an iron bedpost and formed a partial roof to protect Mrs. Mason. Their dog "Shep" had been sleeping in their room and made his way to her side. Undoubtedly the heat of his body helped her to survive. After she had been buried for sixty hours, she was finally removed by the rescue party. She was the only survivor of the disaster.

The rescuers made a sled of sheet iron and pulled Mrs. Mason to the Conway ranch where Dr. Krebs attended her. A few days later she was placed on a toboggan and pulled 16 miles to Bodie by men on skis, the last eight miles up a steep grade. About a week later she was taken by sleigh ten miles and then put in an auto for Thorne, where she was put on the train for Oakland. There she was admitted to Fabiola Hospital, where her right leg was amputated at the knee. It had become infected during the long contact with the dead body of her husband.

The seven people who died in the disaster were buried at Jordan, a short distance north of the wrecked power plant. After Mrs. Mason's recovery, she was employed by the power company for a number of years.

Snow on Bodie's covered sidewalks was sometimes almost enough to prevent the Post Office's couriers from "the swift completion of their appointed rounds."

The stage shown at Yerington, Nevada, was a different type from the Concords that came regularly to Bodie. A few representatives of the younger generation have joined the boys in front of the Commercial saloon, below. The management there seems to have changed sometime between the taking of the picture below and the one on page 136.

The U. S. Hotel, under the management of Mrs. Palmer Miller, was about fifty yards north of the Occidental on the east side of Main Street. Dining rooms in the hotels and boarding houses were well equipped and tables were set with crisp white linen and attended by uniformed maids.

The Standard Consolidated Mining Co.'s Green Creek dam, above, and power plant, below, are shown on this page. Opposite are two impressive pieces of electrical equipment. The three-kilowatt, 500-volt General Electric bipolar motor, above, could run at 700 rpm during its years of service operating equipment at the Standard assay office. Now it is at the Bodie Museum. The G. E. multipolar generator, below, could spin at the same speed, generating 550 volts at 180 amperes. It was used at the substation in the Standard mill, where it remains, idle, to this day. (*Lorena E. Meadows collection, below*)

Snow could be a rugged probem in Bodie at any time. The eight-man crew with Tommy Miller its junior member, left, can well take pride in having cleared the way to the Post Office. The snowy view south on Main Street, below is impressive, but look at the picture next to it and see how things were on March 8, 1911! In those days skis were called "snowshoes." The horse-drawn sleigh took supplies from Bodie to the Mills; Mono Craters rise in the background.

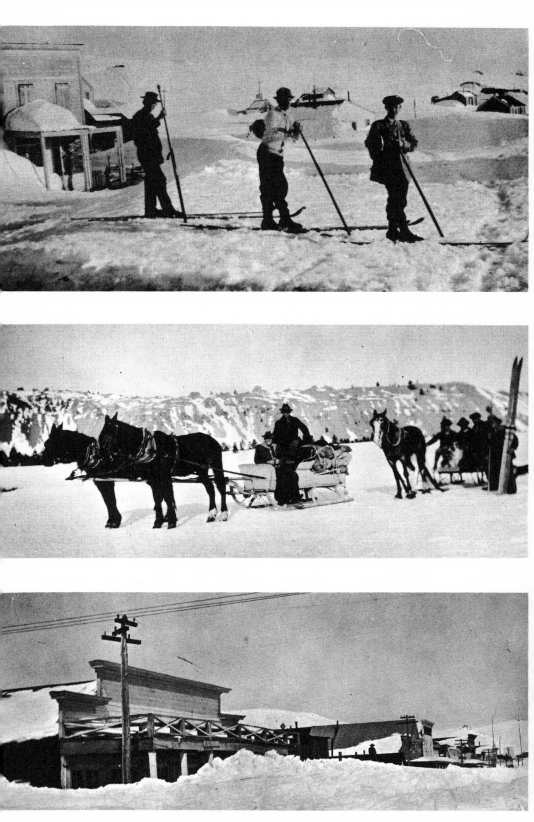

The powerhouse and cottages at Jordan were photographed, above, under construction and before the winter closed in. The roof on the nearer cottage is being shingled. The concrete construction of the powerhouse can be seen in the interior picture, showing the great Pelton wheel and the generator it turned.

The picture above shows the concrete wall slab that saved Mrs. Mason from being crushed by the weight of the snow and the debris of her cottage. In the lower picture is the improvised sheet iron sled on which she reposed when being transported from the ruins of the power plant to the Conway ranch where she rested for several days.

Here is the first auto into Bodie on June 12, 1905. Jim Cain is timing its departure from Bodie for Carson City. The actual running time of the trip turned out to be nine hours. The determined-looking driver is a Mr. Lemmon who is flanked by Dr. Goode, a man "having a reputation for speed," according to George T. Mills, the man at the far side of the back seat, who gazes at the camera past Panama-hatted Mr. Raycraft. The tires show results of contact with rough mountain and desert roads. The rope arrangement on the left front wheel, a common expedient, was a poor substitute for a pneumatic tire.

CHAPTER SIX

THE AUTOMOBILE COMES TO CAMP

i. Motor cars in the West

In 1905 when I arrived in Tonopah the horse was still supreme in transportation. In the more developed parts of the country, where roads were passable and where fuel and service of a sort could be found, the automobile was by no means unknown, although far from common. My years in Tonopah were the years of the coming of automotive transportation to the once-wild West.

The first motor car I can recall seeing in Tonopah was used on the Manhattan stage run. I also remember the Thomas Flyer open touring car with chain drive that came on the Around the World Race in early 1908. It was loaded down with tires, gasoline cans, bedding, shovels, tools, wire, and miscellaneous gear of the sort needed by a car going into territories where the auto had never before traveled.

The arrival of the first car into Bodie was considered such a historical event that the date and occasion were recorded: it came from Carson City on June 12, 1905.

In the early days of undependable cars and trucks traveling on primitive roads with sketchy service facilities, difficulties were great, as will be seen in this chapter. The first automobile roads in the West were the old wagon ruts, some worn so deep that it was necessary to straddle one if the car was not to hang up on the high centers. For years teams and wagons, lurching over the primitive roads, had been dropping miscellaneous debris, including nails, bolts and glass. Consequently the first cars' flimsy tires were repeatedly damaged. Punctures were so common in those days that a twenty-mile trip without one was something to talk about.

As the years went on, vehicles and roads improved, and so did facilities for service along the way; all these made an increasing contribution to the accessibility of the remote camps. They were even able to help with transportation during the severe winters of the region.

Breakdowns on the road were common and one was always wise to take along a man on a trip to help out in case of trouble. Extra spring leaves, spring clips, and — above all — plenty of baling wire were necessary items for repairs. Shaft-driven cars often suffered broken axles, so extra rear axles were generally carried against this emergency. In my car I always carried an extra ring-and-pinion gear for the differential. On a number of occasions I had to replace such items on the road at a considerable distance from help or communication. Garages were unknown.

Tires were usually of the clincher type, 4½ x 37, carrying a pressure of about 75 pounds. A puncture meant dismounting the tire, removing the tube, patching the tube, replacing the tube, remounting the tire and inflating it with an old fashioned hand pump. Your back was sore by the time you had that tire up to the required pressure. They did not give much mileage; a tire that went 1500 to 2000 miles was considered good. In 1916 we considered it phenomenal when a tire on a Hudson went 3500 miles before it finally blew out near Carson City. Besides being undependable, tires were very costly, as much as $72 without tube, in 1915.

Somebody once asked Jim Cain how much it cost to operate his Thomas. Jim thought a moment and then observed that it had four cylinders and that as each cylinder shot, it said "Two bits, four bits, six bits and a dollar!" This wasn't much of an exaggeration.

ii. Bearing troubles

The lumber company had a Thomas Detroit five-passenger touring car during the revival of mining in Aurora. This four cylinder auto was equipped with neither generator nor self-starter and had headlights illuminated by carbide gas.

A connecting rod bearing had failed and been replaced by one we had cast out of bearing metal in Aurora. We were not too sure of it and when we had to take the president of our company, Mr. Charles E. Knox, from Bodie and Aurora to Hawthorne and Thorne to meet the train, I asked our machinist to go along in case we should have trouble. No parts were available nearer than San Francisco.

All went well on the trip with Mr. Knox. He met his train on schedule and we started from Hawthorne on our return trip the following day. We had gone seven miles to the lower Lucky Boy mine and were climbing up the grade when the bearing we had replaced in Aurora was knocked out. Fortunately we were able to coast back to Hawthorne and received permission to work on the car in a blacksmith shop. Although none of the babbits or alloys available in Hawthorne were really suitable to an auto engine, we found some bearing metal which might do, and we had to take a chance on it.

After installing the new bearing, we started out again the following day. With us was another man whom I had hired as a section boss for the Bodie railroad. We went along nicely until we had almost reached the summit 15 miles from Hawthorne and about 4000 feet higher. Here the bearing gave out again. The heat of the sizzling summer day did not help matters at all.

This time we were on a flat from which we could coast in neither direction. For some time we waited in hope that an auto or team would come along to pull us to the summit so we could coast down the other side. Nobody came, and we realized there was nothing for us to do but go to work right there on the road, which was banked on both sides.

We drained the water and oil into cans and spread a canvas under the car. Cans and canvas were always part of the emergency equipment. The only way we could run the car was to remove the piston and connecting rod with its burned-out bearing from the engine. This required removal of the crankcase and the two front cylinders, which were cast in blocks of two. After all this was done, we replaced the engine block, crankcase, oil and water, cranked up and finally got the engine started with the three remaining cylinders operating jerkily but effectively.

It was a rough twenty-mile ride, but we managed to reach Aurora that night. There we left the auto until parts were received from San Francisco. During the whole return trip from Hawthorne, we did not encounter a single car, truck or team.

iii.   Two-time loser

The Standard Mining Co. had an air-cooled Franklin in 1911, for the use of the superintendent. On one of his trips to Reno he passed through Carson City at a greater speed than the gendarmes thought necessary. The superintendent was thereupon brought before the justice of the peace who fined him liberally.

On his return from Reno the superintendent may still have been feeling resentful at being fined; perhaps he was a bit high, as well. North of Carson City he stopped at a ranch and hired a man and team of horses to haul his car through the town, although there was nothing wrong with the machine. He let it be known that he did not want to exceed the speed for that sleepy burg. And as a result he was again hauled before the court and again fined, this time for disturbing the peace.

iv.   Carrying the bullion

When miners get together it is natural for them to discuss their successes and failures. When a leaser sends ore to the mill this becomes a subject of general conversation. From the mill comes a bar of gold bullion which has to be shipped to the mint. With so much value tied up in a bar everybody knows about, there is understandable nervousness about it. In the history of Bodie with its "bad men" and several stage robberies is evidence that this concern was well founded.

In the old days Wells Fargo used to pick up the bullion shipments at Bodie three times a week for many years. The strongbox filled with bullion required two or three men to lift it to the stage. Any shipment valued at over $500 had to be accompanied by a messenger. Two messengers were required if the value exceeded $100,000. One shipment by the Standard Consolidated Mining Co. amounted to half a million dollars and was guarded by six messengers, well armed with shotguns and pistols. Two rode in the stage, the rest went on horseback, two ahead and two behind the stage.

The stage was routed from Bodie to Aurora and on to Fletcher's station. From there it went north via Sweetwater, Wellington and Minden to Carson City. The bullion might be delivered to the mint there or else it would be shipped on to San Francisco.

This era ended in 1912 when Wells Fargo closed its Bodie agency and discontinued the stage route. From then on, the bullion had to go by automobile to the Wells Fargo office in Reno, nearly 150 miles to the north. The cars usually followed much the same route as the old stage coaches, unless there was good reason to vary it.

On one occasion when Jim Cain's son, Jimmy, and I had to take a gold bar worth about $10,000, it seemed prudent to go another way. Strangers of questionable character had recently been seen around Aurora and Bodie and there were rumors of difficulties with them. We decided to go by way of Bridgeport to Sweetwater and thence on to Reno by way of Carson City.

In Nevada at that time, even the important roads were terrible and the main route between the capital and the metropolis of the state was as bad as any. At the hill north of Carson City, the road to Reno branched into a pair of routes, one crossing the west side, and the other the east side, of the Washoe Valley. They rejoined on the hill at the other end. Both were rough dirt roads and it made little difference which one you took. You might decide on either one and be sure it wouldn't be long before you wished you had taken the other.

On this particular occasion Jimmy and I decided to take the branch on the east side of the valley. By the time we had jounced halfway across it a tire had picked up a nail and the engine decided it had had enough. There was nothing for us to do but "get out and get under." It was inconvenient and caused a hazardous delay in the delivery of that bullion, but we had to be prepared for such emergencies in those times. They were all in the day's work.

We had no trouble with bandits, but because of the breakdown we did not reach Reno until after dark, several hours after the Wells Fargo office had closed for the day. The question was what to do with the bullion. Although not a large bar, it was worth $10,000 and we had to keep it safe until the next day when we could turn it over to the express company.

Holdups and burglaries were not uncommon in Reno at that time and we registered in the old Golden Hotel which was not immune from a rash of thievery from its rooms. In ours was a notice to keep the transom over the door closed and the door locked. We heard of instances when the trousers of sleeping occupants were pulled through the transom with a long wire and hook and everything of value removed from the pockets before the pants were dropped on the floor.

Considering the various possibilities of danger, we decided against placing the bar of bullion in the hotel safe and took it to bed with us. Nothing happened to mar our rest and the next morning we were at the Wells Fargo office when it opened. It was with relief that we turned the bullion over to them for shipment to San Francisco.

There may have been little to the rumors and reports of questionable characters on the road and thievery in Reno, but the difficulty with the car and the ensuing delay did nothing to lessen our apprehension. Under these conditions you get an uncomfortable feeling that you are "holding the sack" and you look for the safest way out.

v. The Flivver

The Model T Ford stood up better than other cars under the rigors of early day automobile travel in Mono County. It had its share of troubles, but repairs could be improvised which were impossible on the other cars. Baling wire was a most useful panacea. No Ford owner would have considered going anywhere without this necessity in the tool box.

One of the troubles of the Model T was in the gravity feed of gasoline to the carburetor. This was so high in the engine compartment that fuel from the tank under the front seat would not flow to it on a steep grade, if the tank were more than half empty. To get up such a grade the car had to be turned around and backed up, easier said than done since it was often necessary to back a considerable distance down the grade to find a suitable place to turn the car around.

Gus Hess had a Model T that we often used at Mono Mills. Once we had to abandon it a couple of miles from the camp on account of snow. Three weeks passed before the weather permitted us to return to the machine and try to get it back to the camp. To make matters worse, the tank had been filled with distillate, cheaper than gasoline, but inferior for power and slow starting. We took turns cranking the engine for a couple of hours, to no avail.

We became so disgusted at being unable to start the engine that Gus decided to burn it up. We gathered brush, soaked it with distillate, placed it under the carburetor, lit it and made tracks for the timber, expecting an explosion. It was a nice fire that burned itself out. Nothing more happened and after a wait of half an hour we went back to the machine. On the first turn of the crank the motor started and off we went, back to the camp.

vi. Hunting with speedster

In the late fall wild ducks were plentiful on Mono Lake and the smaller ponds along its east shore near the railroad from Bodie to Mono Mills. Often we would ride the gasoline speedster along the tracks out to the lake to hunt ducks. On one of these trips, I went with C. B. Burkham, who had a general store in Bodie and also ran the stage lines, one of his auto stage drivers, a locomotive engineer and Stuart Cain — not forgetting Brownie, a good hunting dog. After loading guns, ammunition, food and wet goods, we left Bodie in the morning for Warm Springs, 21 miles out. The day was cold, but we were all snug in our ankle-length coats lined with fur and sheepskin.

We had good success in our shooting and, toward dusk, loaded the track car and started back to Bodie. As our speedster had only two seats in front, Burkham, Cain and I sat on the platform in back. All went well until we came to a section of track that passed through a sand cut. The wind had blown hard all day, filling part of the cut and covering the rails. Bill Beaver, the engineer who was operating the car, did not notice the sand as we came around the curve entering the cut and the next thing we knew, the speedster left the track, throwing men, guns, supplies, ducks and dog in all directions. The speedster turned over and lay on its side with the engine running until we shut off the switch. Fortunately the only casualty was Waters, the stage driver, who had bruised his back landing on one of the rails. The dog was sitting on the bank of the sand cut looking very much surprised. A few feet from him lay an unopened bottle of whiskey.

After clearing the sand from the rails, we righted the car and set it on them. All was well with it except that the front axle had sprung, causing a wheel to grind on the frame of the car. We had to take our time for the rest of the trip and finally reached Bodie in the middle of the night.

vii. Five conveyances to Hawthorne

Snow was heavy in Bodie during the winter of 1913-14. My wife was in San Francisco where our son, James W., was born January 19, 1914. Naturally I wanted to get to San Francisco as soon as possible, but Bodie had been snowed in for a week and the only way out was on skis. The nearest place a team from outside could reach was Del Monte, ten miles northeast, where the road branched off to Aurora.

I arranged with the Burkham stage line to hold a team and sleigh there for me and went over the snow from Bodie with one of our men. It was heavy going with suitcases on our backs. The snow stuck to our skis, but we finally made it by sundown. My companion continued on to Aurora, two miles farther, while the team took me to Fletcher station, 16 miles from Bodie, to spend the night.

The following morning we started out from Fletcher's with a wagon, as the snow was lighter at the lower elevation; but before going over Lucky Boy Pass on the way to Hawthorne, the team had to change to a sleigh once more. The stage line had left one by the road there for that purpose. This took us over the summit and several miles on the other side to a place near upper Lucky Boy. Here we were met by an auto stage that had brought mail and parcel post from Hawthorne. This was transferred to the driver with the team to take back to Fletcher station, while the auto took me to Hawthorne where I spent the night.

The next morning the auto took me the half-dozen miles from Hawthorne to Thorne, Nevada, where I met the train for San Francisco. Thus in 45 miles I had used five conveyances — skis, sleigh, wagon, sleigh again and auto — to reach the train for San Francisco.

viii. Through the snow to Minden

Women needed much fortitude to live in mining camps. This was true in the days of the Forty Niners; it was just as true in the later mining camps, when they were just developing or when they were practically abandoned. There was plenty for a woman to worry about: Few neighbors, lack of transportation in winter with below-zero temperatures and heavy snow, lack of doctors or medical facilities except what might be on hand at home.

I will never forget a trip my wife had to endure early in January, 1917, when she was pregnant. She and her mother were planning to go from Bodie to San Francisco, by auto to Hawthorne and the rest of the way by train. Just when they were about to leave, a heavy snowfall delayed their departure for several days. Stages suspended service between Bodie and Hawthorne. The planned trip by auto and train turned into something quite different.

We finally decided to take a team with bob sleigh for my wife and son, Bill, along with her mother, my brother, another man and myself. Women in those days, of course, did not travel with small suitcases and light clothes, so we also had trunks of clothing along with other baggage. The sleigh was heavily loaded. We started for Aurora where, we had been assured, an auto was available to take us on to Reno.

The snow was deep and high winds had drifted it so badly that several times the sleigh was in danger of turning over and spilling us all on the snow. It took us some time to travel the four miles to the Gregory ranch where we were grateful for the opportunity to warm up for the trip ahead. Six miles farther, at Del Monte, we noticed that the snow on the ground was light enough that an automobile could operate. It became much deeper in the next two miles and Aurora was heavily blanketed. There we were made comfortable in the Cain residence.

Although the camp was rapidly being abandoned, several men joined us the next morning. The only automobile in town was a five-passenger Buick touring car owned by the foreman of the crew dismantling the stamp mill. He was anxious to get it out of Aurora and store it at Del Monte where he could make use of it. Unfortunately the snow was too deep for it to move. We all joined forces and cleared the road enough so that the team of horses could pull the car from Aurora to Del Monte. This took a couple of days. Finally we were ready to resume the journey.

My wife and her mother were getting anxious with the delays. At last we again loaded the sleigh with passengers, trunks and all for the two-mile trip to Del Monte. Most of us piled into the Buick, which had been pulled there the previous day, and rode the twenty miles to Sweetwater. My brother followed with a team and wagon which carried the trunks and other baggage. Meanwhile, I arranged with a rancher to take us to Minden the next day, via Wellington, Mountain House, and Gardnerville.

That day's trip, too, was slow, particularly at Mountain House, where chains were needed on the wheels. Finally we reached Minden, where the folks had to spend another night in the Minden Hotel. Next morning we boarded the Virginia & Truckee train for Reno and checked the baggage through to San Francisco. I returned to Sweetwater with the rancher and then continued with my brother on the return trip to Aurora and Bodie.

I expected to follow my family to San Francisco shortly, but before I could leave Bodie I received a message announcing the arrival of my son Robert on January 13, and that all was well.

ix.   The big Duplex

The power company was doing a lot of development and construction work at Silver Lake and Lee Vining Creek Canyon, as well as at Saddleback Lake on the top of Tioga Pass. They shipped their materials to Benton and we were able to haul a considerable amount as freight on our Duplex trucks.

We made a test trip with a four-ton load to the top of Tioga Pass at an elevation of nearly 10,000 feet. This was the first trip by a loaded truck at the summit of the Tioga Grade, which was then very narrow with short, sharp turns. Our Duplex truck was hard to handle with its long steering radius and had to be backed up the turns before they could be negotiated. At the top of the grade it was a matter of a few inches to stay on the road, while the bed of the truck rubbed the cliffs on the inner side. The solid rubber tires set up a vibration that threatened to start rock slides that would tear out the road.

We finally realized that the big Duplex was impractical and dangerous on the Tioga grade. Subsequently the power company used lighter trucks with pneumatic tires for this work.

We had a different sort of trouble when one of these trucks was climbing a grade in the canyon along Rush Creek. Heavy thunderstorms had brought heavy rain and presently the truck started to skid. Deep ruts kept it from leaving the road and the wheel did not seem to be sinking in the mud, but for some reason it could not get traction. When we investigated we found that a short stretch of the road was densely covered with a mass of polliwogs. The truck could not proceed because its wheels were spinning on them. At this point the road was elevated some distance above Rush Creek. Apparently the tadpoles had been lifted from some pool by the storm and deposited on the road. It was some time before the road was clear enough for the truck to proceed.

x. Influenza

The great influenza epidemic of 1917-18 reached its peak after lumbering operations at Mono Mills had been shut down for the season. There were six men still at the Mills finishing up work there. One of them went to Bishop on business and returned a few days later with a bad cold. Within a few days five of the crew were confined to their beds with the 'flu and the only one to administer to them was the clerk at the store.

When I heard of their sickness I drove to Mono Mills with a team to take a supply of quinine, medicines and a case of whiskey. The clerk gave his patients a steady dose of quinine and whiskey and kept himself well-dosed to ward off the sickness. The men all recovered in a matter of weeks, though some had been seriously ill. Fortunately the clerk remained on his feet throughout, although even he was a bit shaky at times.

xi. Selling war bonds and stamps

During the first World War, I was appointed to a committee for the sale of War Savings Bonds and Stamps in Mono County. With my colleagues, Jim Cain and Judge Pat R. Parker, we set out in Cain's 1916 Hudson Super Six to cover the county. Over long stretches of old country road we traveled to isolated ranches and communities, many miles apart. I don't believe we missed a ranch or inhabitant in the whole county, including many Indians.

It took some time for us to do the job and one of our last stops was at the old Filosena ranch in Mono Basin. Mrs. Filosena contributed generously, as did all the others, and to make the necessary payments, she went to her "safe deposit" under the mattress.

As we were ready to leave for Bridgeport, we noticed several suckling pigs in the Filosena's sty. Judge Parker thought that one of these would be just the thing to grace the table at his home for a dinner celebrating completion of our job.

Georgie Filosena climbed over the fence to catch one of the little pigs while his mother went to get a barley sack for it. Soon Georgie came back over the fence with a squealing pig and dropped it into the sack which his mother was holding open. The pig went into the sack and right through the open bottom to the ground. Quick as a flash it scampered away into the sagebrush. Unfortunately no one had thought to check the sack's bottom. We decided to look elsewhere for our dinner.

Our drive succeeded in going over the quota assigned to us and Mono County soon had a flag to show for it.

Dolly Cain looks incredibly cool and immaculate at the wheel of the smooth-tired automobile in Aurora.

Bert Lundy's sporty Doris (all three views) seems like a sassy intruder into the Sierra grandeur that surrounds the village of Lundy.

An older and more dependable means of motive power comes to the rescue of the disabled early model automobile somewhere in the desert, above. Like the cars on the three preceding pages, it used the public roads in the days before a license plate was required. That situation had changed by 1918 when we wrecked our Pope-Hartford, coming down the grade from Mono Lake summit. Nat Smith and Art Murphy are looking it over and I was behind the camera. We were coming to Bodie from Mono Mills where we had been pulling up the railroad tracks.

Here is another view of our beautifully crafted but unfortunate Pope-Hartford. I'm in this one and the camera is manned by Nat. We knew we were lucky to get off as well as we did, considering the speed we had been going. That's why we all look so happy in these pictures. Sometime during the World War I years the Gilkey stage, below, turned over on the Lucky Boy grade between Hawthorne and Bodie. The people in the picture seem to have survived the accident in good shape.

Moyle Gilkey organized a stage line between Bodie and Hawthorne in about 1914. In the picture above we see it about to leave Bodie on its first trip. It ran competition to Cecil Burkham's auto mail and stage line, shown below arriving at Burkham's store in Bodie.

All I can say about those hats, above, is that the ladies actually wore them when they went motoring. That Mitchell car in front of the Cain house in Bodie was as much of a beauty in its way as Dolly Cain, who was at the wheel. Look at the length of that hood, the brass radiator with its sculpture, the headlamp and the bulb-operated horn with its long coiled air tube. Next to Dolly is Jessie Bell; the girl in back is Verna Sturgeon. Our Oldsmobile track auto wasn't elegant, but it was fun. I'm at the wheel, sitting next to Gus Hess; his brother Will is sitting on the back and Frank Olaqua stands behind.

On these pages are five examples of automotive elegance around the year 1910. In the Thomas Flyer, above, it is easy to see how the ladies kept their formidable headgear in place through the jolts and breezes of a ride in an open car over rough desert roads. Below we see a sporty white Thomas roadster and a Simplex in front of Hammond's store by Mono Lake.

In the woods near Silver Lake, above, is a Hudson Super Six touring car, the windshield open to admit the bracing mountain air. The big seven passenger Thomas, below, has apparently detoured around a stalled hay wagon. It is probably the same car as the one at the top of the other page. Its occupants, in their militaristic headgear, have gotten out to look over the situation.

Those early cars all had right-hand drive. I am the passenger in Gould Reading's Mitchell while he is at the wheel. Below it is a seven passenger Thomas touring car parked in front of the Aurora Post office in 1911. Jim Cain is standing on the other side of the car's hood. A spare tube is draped around the parking lamp. At the bottom of the other page, perhaps in Bodie, is Judge Campbell who took part in the Yribarren case mentioned in Chapter II. Leaning over in the back seat is my boss, Charles E. Knox. Above is Jim Cain's splendid Thomas parked before the Aurora Post Office, with an eagle mounted on the brass radiator. Arthur Murphy, with the goggles, leans against the wheel. Jimmie Cain, in his linen suit, sits at the wheel; his mother stands behind the hood and my wife Dolly stands in the doorway, holding our oldest son. In contrast to these well-dressed folk, Joe Fanger looks every bit the working man, seated at the wheel of the Thomas-Detroit touring car in the 1912 scene at Mono Mills, below.

The black car on the lonely desert hillside, above, is Stuart Cain's 1916 Hudson Super Six. At the top of the other page, Lester E. Bell stands beside the Model T Ford; the picture is labeled "Grandpa and his Ford." The spare tire has apparently been put to use and one hopes that Grandpa will not immediately have another puncture. At the bottom of these pages the solid tired, four-wheel drive Duplex truck appears in two different uses, about 1921 in Bodie.

Above is the 1916 Hudson Super Six we used in our Mono County tour, selling War Savings bonds and stamps. The 1934 model station wagon fitted out for traction in the snow belonged to the Roseklip Co. It is shown in front of Stuart Cain's garage in Bridgeport.

These ponderous Best caterpillar tractors passed through Mono Mills in 1915, carrying supplies from Benton station, on the Southern Pacific's Carson & Colorado narrow gauge branch, to Silver Lake, on Rush Creek in the Sierra Nevada southwest of Mono Lake. There, the Duncanson-Harrelson Co. of San Francisco was building a power plant and dams for the Pacific Power Co., which became California Electric Co. and now is part of Southern California Edison. They could haul twenty-ton loads.

The Treadwell-Yukon Co plant, above, was treating mine dumps and surface ground when the picture above was taken in 1930. By July, 1942, the Roseklip Co. had built and was operating the mill in the picture below for the same purpose. The view looks north from the Goodshaw mine. The dark building in the right foreground is the old railroad office.

CHAPTER SEVEN

QUIET YEARS AT BODIE

i. Dismantling the railroad

With the closing down of the mines in Aurora and the lull in mining activities at Bodie and Masonic, demand for lumber and cordwood greatly diminished and the lumber company had to cease operations. To pay off indebtedness the railroad was dismantled and the rails and equipment were sold. In all there were about 38 miles of the three-foot gauge track.

I had the contract for taking up the rails and delivering them to Mono Mills, along with spikes and plates. Gus Hess, who had served the company ably for many years as blacksmith and mechanic in the Mono Mills shop, was in charge of the dismantling crew. Work began late in July, 1918.

We took up the tracks, beginning at the Bodie end, and delivered them to Mono Mills. From there they were shipped by truck to Benton station to be loaded on the narrow gauge cars of the Southern Pacific "Slim Princess," formerly the Carson & Colorado. At Owenyo, California, they were transferred to the S. P.'s broad gauge cars for San Francisco where they were shipped to Hawaii, the Philippines and the Orient.

In all we shipped about 2300 tons of 35- and 40-ton rail, along with scrap iron and steel from the dismantled locomotives and cars. The job of dismantling the railroad took us less than two months.

Meanwhile another contractor was hauling the rails from Mono Mills to Benton with five fine new Kleiber trucks. All went well at first, but the trucks, heavily laden with thirty-foot lengths of rail, extending far ahead and behind, greatly overtaxed the primitive road. Chuckholes quickly developed in the volcanic ash; the trucks bounced heavily so that spring shackles would turn over and lock the steering gear. This would stall a truck until help arrived to jack it up and release the springs. Sometimes it was necessary to unload the truck before repairs could be made. Then there remained the task of reloading.

The delays were costly, for the rails could not be delivered to San Francisco on schedule. By the time hauling had to be discontinued on account of snow, half the tonnage still waited, stacked at Mono Mills.

The next season I was asked to take the contract to finish the hauling. Stuart Cain and I took the job, using his two Duplex four-wheel-drive trucks. Instead of loading the rails on the truck beds, we built two-wheel trailers with a bunker on the truck bed, so the seven-ton loads of rails were evenly distributed. We kept an Indian crew on the road to make repairs and to fill in the chuckholes with sagebrush as they developed.

With modern high-speed motors, today's cars and trucks would have had a hard time negotiating the roads of that era. Wheels would have spun in the dust and loose gravel that were then so prevalent. This was less of a problem for the older engines with their lower speeds.

ii. Departure from Bodie

After this work was completed Guss Hess moved to Tioga Lodge, the new name for Hammond's Station, on Mono Lake, where he opened a repair shop. He later moved to a ranch where with Chris Mattly and one or two others he established the community of Lee Vining on Highway 395 south of Mono Lake and at the eastern end of the Tioga grade.

Meanwhile in 1918, with Victor Cain and George Denham, I secured a lease on the mine dumps of the Standard property. We dismantled the old South End cyanide plant and reconstructed it near the Bodie Mine shaft. We added crushing rolls and other equipment. The plant operated on a small scale for a couple of years. It was the first serious attempt to mine and treat the dumps and surface ground. It helped to establish the mineral values of this material and the necessity for a large-capacity plant with modern machinery and equipment.

Lacking the capital for this sort of development and seeing a rather restricted future in Bodie otherwise, I moved to San Francisco with my wife and family in 1920. There I soon entered the employ of the Pacific Gas & Electric Co., an association that was to endure for thirty years, the last 15 of which was in the capacity of assistant treasurer.

Jim Cain remained in Bodie, looking after his bank and many other interests there, including the mine properties many of which were being operated by leasers. In the early 1920s his wife came to San Francisco and made her home with us. He continued to live in the family home in Bodie with his son Victor and Victor's family. He kept the Bodie Bank open all through the quiet 1920s and into the 1930s.

iii.   Leasing at Broken Hills

Even the interest in my new work with P. G. & E. could not take away my interest in Bodie, Mono County, and the desert mining regions generally. Early in 1926 I joined with some friends in taking a lease on mining property in the Broken Hills Mining District in Churchill County, about 63 miles east of Fallon, Nevada.

The district had been discovered in 1913. While no great activity resulted, a settlement sprang up and some work was carried on into the early 1920s. The camp was situated in a dry, desolate desert area, 12 miles from the nearest water. The rough desert road was dusty and strewn with rocks. The "town" of Broken Hills consisted of four or five small frame cabins dating from the original 1913 discovery. It had almost vanished by the time we were working the property.

Suddenly Broken Hills was again swarming with activity when a strike of rich silver ore was reported in the Quartz Mountain mine, a couple of miles to the east. Quite a few prospectors and mining men came in and located claims in all directions, mostly on the basis of wild hopes. Tents and temporary shacks appeared. An enterprising man set up a "service station" consisting of a couple of fifty-gallon barrels of gasoline and a case of oil in quart cans. This was shielded from the hot desert sun by a piece of canvas stretched from four posts. Needless to say, anyone needing gas and oil had to pay a good price, but people were glad enough to get it.

Several times I went to the camp from San Francisco to look after the work on our lease. I considered myself fortunate that Fred Ross, one of the owners of the mining property we were leasing, invited me to stay in a cabin which belonged to his sister-in-law, a Mrs. Daniels of Hawthorne, Nevada.

Once I went there with one of our partners, a young man who had never experienced the rigors and conditions of a mining camp. We left San Francisco early in the morning and arrived at Broken Hills about midnight, after several long detours. Mrs. Daniels was in the cabin when we arrived and showed us to our quarters in the room between the front room, where she was to sleep, and the kitchen in the rear.

We retired, but about two in the morning I was aroused by someone knocking on the front door. It was a deputy sheriff who was having trouble with a "lady of the evening." She had been the center of some commotion among her gentlemen friends. The deputy told Mrs. Daniels that he needed help in taking care of his prisoner until he could get her to jail in Fallon in the morning. In the meantime would Mrs. Daniels take her in for the rest of the night!

When I heard what was going on I awakened my partner. "Pete," I said, "it looks as if she will have to crawl in bed with you and I will have to sit up in the kitchen the rest of the night."

Pete heatedly declared that he would stand for no such arrangement. He finally calmed down when Mrs. Daniels announced that the gal would sleep with her.

These trips to Broken Hills often included visits to Bodie. One time Mrs. Daniels rode with me as far as her home in Hawthorne. As we approached her town we noticed a dark cloud of smoke over it. Drawing closer, we could at last see the building that was on fire.

"Look," exclaimed Mrs. Daniels, "The hotel! Just imagine all the bed bugs that are burning up!"

Having spent a night in that hotel, I knew Mrs. Daniels was right.

As recently as June 4, 1965, on a trip with Don Segerstrom, I decided to see what was left of the old camp at Broken Hills. Much to my surprise we found three of the old frame cabins still standing, rather caved in, including the one that belonged to Mrs. Daniels. The old headframe was still upright over the shaft of the Broken Hills mine. The only sad note was a lonely grave surrounded by an iron fence on top of a small mound just off the old road. The stone marked the spot where an old prospector named Costello had been buried several years before, as he had requested.

iv. Prohibition at Bodie

The 1920s were the years of the "Great Experiment, Noble in Purpose." An old mining camp with the traditions of Bodie did not, of course, take kindly to such an experiment, and various methods were used to circumvent the law. A pair of bootleggers worked out a plan suited to the nearly deserted old camp.

In the cemetery was a headstone adorned with a pair of iron plates bearing the name and particulars of the deceased. Four bolts passing through the hollow headstone anchored the front plate to the back one. Between the two plates was space large enough to hold several bottles of liquor.

The supplier would visit the grave, remove the back plate, take the money left there by the purchaser, put the bottled goods in the opening and replace the iron plate. At the proper time the buyer would visit the grave to remove his supply of thirst-quencher.

After Repeal there were noticeably fewer mourners visiting the cemetery.

v. Peg leg tragedy

One night in the late 1920s I was in Bodie, conferring with Jim Cain on some business matters, in the back office of the bank. At about 9 p.m. one of the tough characters of the town, the man named Sam, came into the bank. He had been drinking and was in a quarrelsome mood. He started an argument with me that made no sense and very nearly ended in a fight. I remember Jim Cain picking up the poker from the stove to use if things got out of hand. Sam was a strong, husky man and I would probably have needed a little help.

Fortunately, Sam suddenly quieted down a bit and tried to tell me something about helping him with a man who had been injured. After a little time and prodding we finally learned the story.

Louie Levine, an old timer in the camp, had long ago lost a leg and for years had gotten around town well on a peg leg. This evening, walking down the wooden sidewalk in the dark, he had accidentally put his peg leg into a large knothole in one of the boards. The sidewalk was elevated at that point and the peg leg went all the way down the hole to the knee, crushing the stump end of Louie's leg badly.

Sam had helped Levine back to his room in the brick building on Main Street, next to the Odd Fellows Hall, but could not find anyone else to help him, perhaps on account of his intoxicated condition; so he called on me. With the matter explained, I agreed to go with Sam and see what could be done. Cautiously, I told Sam to walk up the dark street ahead of me and things quieted down considerably.

When we arrived at Levine's room, we took off the peg leg and dressed the crushed stump as best we could. No doctor was available and I asked Sam to stay with Louie the rest of the night. The next morning we placed Levine in my auto and I took him to the County Farm where a doctor from nearby Bridgeport attended him.

Louie did not last long. He was along in years and the shock and injury were too much for him.

vi. Decline and fires

Through the 1920s leasers operated the mining properties in Bodie. In 1928 the Clinton-West Co. operated the dumps and surface ground of Jim Cain's properties, while the Old

Gold Mining Co. operated and unwatered the Red Cloud shaft of the Southern Consolidated Co. Late in 1929 the Treadwell-Yukon Co. took over the lease of both properties. It continued its mining operations until December 1931, when they were closed down under the financial strain of the great Depression.

Meanwhile the old camp continued to sleep under its heavy blanket of snow in the winters and to doze in the hot sun of the Mono County summers. Jim Cain and a very few other people continued to live where thousands had once experienced the strenuous activity of a booming mining town. Each morning he would open the doors of his bank whether any customers were in prospect or not.

In the summer of 1932, June 23, a destructive fire wiped out most of the town including Jim Cain's bank, but not including his home nor the one where I had lived. While the contents of the bank vault were safe, the bank did not reopen. Jim remained in town until 1935, when he leased his mining properties to the Roseklip Co. Then he came to San Francisco where he opened an office and joined his wife living with us.

The Roseklip Co. practically rebuilt the plant for the treatment of the mine dumps and the surface ground. They operated until 1942 when operations were discontinued under the gold restrictions. At that time they had been treating 500 tons a day. In 1946 they started to recondition the plant to resume operations, but before this was finished the plant was completely destroyed by fire. No operations of consequence have been carried on at Bodie since then. Eight years later the big Standard cyanide plant was also destroyed by fire.

vii.   Sam Leon visits the City

During the later years in Bodie there was a small lunch counter and saloon, jokingly referred to as the "Bodie Night Club." It was operated by a Chinese Mono County resident of long standing. Sam Leon had worked as a cook, a miner and on other jobs, mostly in mining camps.

In about 1936 he had a lease in the old Bodie Mine where he found some good milling ore which was treated in the Standard Mill and the bullion was shipped to the San Francisco Mint by the Cain Company. Jim Cain was by then in San Francisco, living with my wife and me, and was advised that Sam would call on him at his office to receive his share of the bullion proceeds.

One morning while I was in my office at the Pacific Gas & Electric Co. in San Francisco, a clerk came to my room and told me there was a gentleman in the main office to see me.

I followed her to see who wanted to see me, and was greeted with a boisterous "Hello!" from Sam Leon. With him were his Paiute squaw and two small children. After greetings all around, he explained that he had come to the City to show his family the sights and to pick up his check from Mr. Cain. Not knowing where to find him, he had called on me.

After much loud talk, describing his trip and the excitement of his family, he left with my directions to Mr. Cain's office. The last I saw of Sam and his family, they were walking up Market Street, single file, with Sam in the lead, followed by his wife and the two children. Such a procession was not unheard of in San Francisco, but it was not usual either and the office force chided me about my unusual acquaintances.

Jim Cain was in his San Francisco office that day, but not many years more, for in 1939, at the age of 84, this pioneer Western businessman, fifty years in Bodie, my friend and father-in-law died. Mrs. Cain followed him in 1943.

viii. "Ghost town" Bodie

Most of Bodie had burned down. The camp's foremost businessman and booster was gone. Although a very large tonnage of valuable ore remained in the mine dumps and surface ground of the Standard property, the closing of operations in 1942 under the "gold clause" postponed any hope of cashing in on this ore. Efforts to rehabilitate the Roseklip cyanide mill following World War II were cut short when the mill burned down in 1946, ending the last large-scale effort to process the ore. Probably only a change in economic conditions and a justified rise in the price of gold will bring the mining industry back to Bodie.

I retired from the P. G. & E. in 1950, after which I devoted considerable time to clearing up the wreckage of old mills in Bodie. Much usable machinery was salvaged and sold to operations elsewhere. After 1954 I negotiated for the J. S. Cain Co. with the State of California for the inclusion of Bodie in the state park system.

After the mines ceased operations, Bodie became famous as a so-called "ghost town" and was often visited by tourists and sightseers. Many of these people were tempted by the furniture, artifacts and equipment that had been left in so many of the unoccupied buildings. These things had been left behind by people departing Bodie to seek employment elsewhere, not because they wished to abandon their property, but simply because of the high cost of transporting goods out of this remote place. Many visitors to the "ghost town" seemed to think that this material did not belong to anyone and could be taken with impunity; they did not hesitate to break into buildings for this purpose.

The Cain Company watchman was kept busy the year round, but especially in the school vacation periods and the tourist season. Some things taken as souvenirs were ridiculous, while other thefts were of a nature not usually associated with sightseeing trips. Windows and doors were deliberately broken, even though in many cases they had been left unlocked for easy entry.

Carelessness on the part of tourists occasionally resulted in fires. This is the most likely cause of a spectacular fire which destroyed the old Standard cyanide mill in July of 1954. It did not take the flames long to consume this wooden structure with corrugated iron siding.

The big bell on the roof of the firehouse of Main Street was a temptation to visitors. Once it was removed and carted away, although it weighed over 200 pounds. Fortunately someone noted the license number of the vehicle and reported it to the sheriff. The car was traced to Long Beach, California, where the bell was found. It was brought back to Bodie and once more mounted on the firehouse roof.

Late one summer evening a couple of years later, when I was visiting Bridgeport, the sheriff received a telephone call from the watchman at Bodie. Somebody had been caught trying to take that bell again. The deputy invited me to go with him and we reached the old camp at about the same time as the Highway Patrol car from Lee Vining, which had also been alerted.

We found a car backed up to the firehouse and two sheepish men were receiving tongue-lashings from their wives. Grimly watching them were Bodie's only two inhabitants, the watchman and an old-time resident who spent the summer there. Both were armed.

These people had come over from Nevada for a picnic and were tempted by the sight of the bell on the firehouse. Under cover of darkness they hoped to load it in their car and get away from the camp without being seen. Unfortunately for their plans, but fortunately for Bodie, they accidentally dropped the bell on the ground with a resounding clang that awakened the watchman and the old resident. Had they thought to muffle the clapper, they might have avoided the attention of the Bodie pair and succeeded in the theft.

They had to follow the sheriff's car to Bridgeport and were in turn followed by the vigilant Highway Patrol car. We reached the county seat by about half past two in the morning and took them to the office of the justice of the peace, who appeared in pajamas and robe to hear the case. It did not take long to hear the evidence and the judge promptly fined the principals $200 plus expenses of the travel by the police cars and the cost of repairing one of the bell hangers which was broken in the fall. He also ordered them not to visit Mono County again for some time under penalty of arrest. They readily agreed to this, for they had seen quite enough of Mono County that night.

The case was closed and the last heard from these people was the tirade of the wives against their penitent husbands.

The picnic had been expensive, but it also tended to deter others from attempting to help themselves to whatever might take their fancy in Bodie, as the word spread that the law was firm in dealing with such offenders.

It is beyond understanding what people will do. The cemeteries have been desecrated, headstones removed from the graves and hauled away. Quite a number of caskets for children have been stolen from the building used as a mortuary. Recently two men drove their pickup truck to the cemetery and unloaded a "scope," an electrical device for locating metals buried in the ground. When the caretaker asked their intentions, they said they were going to go over the graves with the "scope" trying to locate guns that might have been buried with the deceased. They said they had had some success in other old cemeteries and thought the one in Bodie might be promising in this respect. They were ordered off the premises and out of town.

All the so-called "ghost towns" experience this type of vandalism, and if not protected would be carted away. This is what happened to the old camp of Aurora, 12 miles from Bodie. Most of the buildings there were of brick. Everything movable was hauled away and finally the brick buildings themselves were torn down and the bricks hauled off to places in Nevada and California where fine recently-constructed brick buildings are now noticeable.

The old court house, a two-story building erected in the 1860s when Aurora was thought to be in California and was county seat of Mono County, suffered this fate, as did the Masonic Hall, store buildings and others. At least ten brick buildings were torn down and the bricks removed, as there were no residents or caretakers in the old camp. The owners of the buildings, on which they paid taxes, were not aware of the destruction until nearly all the bricks were gone.

The J. S. Cain Co., which owned most of the mines in the Bodie Mining District, and the town itself, maintained the place and had a caretaker on the premises for years before and after the mining operations were shut down under the 1942 gold restrictions. The caretaker was duly deputized by the Mono County Sheriff. This attention, perhaps together with the fact that few of the Bodie buildings were constructed of a material as valuable as brick, served to spare this camp from the wholesale destruction that was visited on its Nevada neighbor.

ix. Bodie State Historical Park

As highways improved and the population of the West increased, more and more tourists and sightseers came to visit Bodie, and with them an increasing danger of vandalism. General interest in the old place and a wish to preserve it for future generations led to the proposal that the town, its buildings and their contents should be included as a historical monument in the California state park system. In 1954 I accompanied Donald I. Segerstrom of Sonora and several representatives of the Division of Beaches and Parks, Department of Natural Resources, on a visual inspection tour of Bodie. The state reached an agreement with the Cain interests and in 1956 Governor Goodwin J. Knight signed an appropriation bill passed by the Legislature.

In June, 1962, the first state park ranger, Jack Evans, arrived to undertake the protection of the town and property. Additional personnel soon came, including Norman Cleaver, park supervisor from 1962 until 1966, when he was succeeded by Robert B. Frenzel.

On September 12, 1964 dedication ceremonies where held at Bodie and four plaques on stone monuments were unveiled. One of them designated the camp as a National Historic Site, the second as a State Historical Landmark. The third, on the site of the Bodie Bank, was in memory of James S. Cain. The fourth was erected by the E Clampus Vitus organization in appreciation of those who had an active part in bringing about the preservation of the town for future generations.

The Bodie of the 1860s, the 1870s and the booming 1880s is but a memory. The bad men from Bodie are long dead. The "man for breakfast" tradition has become part of the lore of the wild West. Jim Cain is gone. The railroad is no more, nor will one ever be needed again to bring timber to Bodie's treeless plain, in these days of smooth roads and efficient trucks. The mines are shut down, but still there, with an unknown quantity of rich ore still locked in the earth until a time when it may once more be feasible to mine it and refine it. If this day comes, the whole operation will be so different from the old frontier days of Bodie that it will be part of a new age.

Meanwhile the site, the relics, the remains and the ruins of the old Bodie are maintained by the State of California so that people of the present and future generations may have a chance to get a glimpse of the colorful life of an age they never knew first hand.

The Miners Union Hall now serves as a museum for Bodie. Here are displayed many such objects as the old-time hearse, gold scales, sewing machine, saddle and flag.

The Inyo was last used in
1918 when it came time to
pull up the tracks over which
it had once hauled timber
from Mono Mills to the mines
of Bodie.

The mule, above, is about to haul tailings for treatment in the Standard cyanide plant. We built the flat-roofed structure, below in 1918, to process material from the dumps we had leased after dismantling the railroad.

I took these pictures of the "boom town" at Broken Hills, Nevada, in 1926. The "service station," below, didn't look like much, but we were glad to have it handy, just the same.

The San Rafael Mining Co. property, top, left, was at Quartz Mountain, near Broken Hills. Above is a view of the Broken Hills mine in May, 1926. I am the one in the cap; at my right is Mr. Broad; to my left are Fred Ross and Charlie Vann. Below is the same mine as it appeared in 1965. The middle picture on the other page shows the tents and shacks where people lived at Broken Hills in 1926. The 1965 view, below it, is of Mrs. Daniels' house where, 39 years earlier, I spent an eventful night.

Somebody stole the epitaph plates that used to be bolted to the front
and back of this cast-iron gravestone in the Bodie cemetery. In the 1966
view, above, it is easy to see that there was plenty of room inside for the
bootleggers to hide bottles of forbidden booze during prohibition years.
Bodie's big 1932 fire did a pretty thorough job of burning the north end
of Main Street, but the vault of Jim Cain's Bodie Bank protected its
contents. There it stands amid the ruins at the bottom of the other page.
(*Three fire pictures: Frasher's Fotos, Pomona, Calif.*)

"BODIE AFIRE" JUNE 23, 1932
BODIE, MONO COUNTY, CALIF.

The Roseklip mill was changed a number of times. From 1935 to 1942 it appeared as in the picture above. The surface materials it treated were collected as shown below.

By 1952 Bodie had taken on the aspect of a ghost town. From the burned ruins of the Roseklip mill, above, equipment was removed for salvage. Below, tourists gaze in the windows of the former rooming house that later was operated as a cafe and saloon.

BODIE

GOLD WAS DISCOVERED HERE IN 1859 BY W. S. BODEY AFTER WHOM THE TOWN WAS NAMED. ONCE THE MOST THRIVING METROPOLIS OF THE MONO COUNTRY, BODIE'S MINES PRODUCED GOLD VALUED AT MORE THAN 100 MILLION DOLLARS. TOUGH AS NAILS, "THE BAD MAN FROM BODIE" STILL CARRIES HIS GUNS AND BOWIE KNIFE DOWN THROUGH THE PAGES OF WESTERN HISTORY.

CALIFORNIA REGISTERED HISTORICAL LANDMARK NO. 341

PLAQUE PLACED BY THE CALIFORNIA STATE PARK COMMISSION IN COOPERATION WITH THE MONO COUNTY DEPARTMENT OF PARKS AND RECREATION AND THE MONO COUNTY HISTORICAL SOCIETY. SEPTEMBER 12, 1964

A spectacular event during Bodie's years as a ghost town was the big fire in July, 1954 at the Standard cyanide mill, opposite. The plaque above and the one on the next page were dedicated in the September 1964 ceremonies, below. The view is toward the east, past the Bodie school house on the left, and toward the old railroad office which is visible just above the ridge above the U.S. flag.

IN GRATITUDE

TO THOSE CLAMPERS AND OTHERS WHO GAVE
UNSTINTINGLY OF THEIR TIME AND ENERGIES TO
MAKE POSSIBLE THE PRESERVATION OF BODIE
AS A MONUMENT TO OUR PIONEER HERITAGE.
ESPECIALLY TO

SEN. PAUL LUNARDI AND EMIL W. BILLEB

AND TO

GOV. E. G. BROWN
LT. GOV. G. M. ANDERSON
HUGO FISHER
C. A. DeTURK
E. F. DOLDER
E. P. HANSON
SEN. CHAS. BROWN
SEN. AL EARHART
SEN. CLAIR ENGLE
N. B. DRURY
E. C. POWELL
A. J. STERN
C. C. FLEHARTY
MARGARET OWINGS
S. S. CRAMER
J. P. ELSBACH
D. A. HOLWAY
H. L. ZELLERBACH
BOBBY BELL
TRACY FAMILY
EARL BELL
J. R. KNOWLAND
P. E. SLOANE

A. D. STEVENOT
V. A. NEASHAM
C. L. NEWLIN
J. DYSON
N. J. CLEAVER
J. N. ROSEKRANS
R. S. DOLLAR, JR.
H. G. HOOVER
D. L. SEGERSTROM
M. M. WHITTAKER
D. V. CAIN
D. V. CAIN, JR.
S. W. CAIN
SEN. WMY SYMONS, JR.
GEO. DELURY, JR.
N. E. DENTON
FRED GARNER
W. R. EVANS
A. G. MAHAN
B. K. FALCONER
W. E. EARWAKER
W. B. CAIN
DR. AL SHUMATE

J. H. MICHAEL

". . . AND TO THE MANY OTHERS WHO GAVE
ENCOURAGEMENT THIS MARKER IS DEDICATED
THIS 12TH DAY OF SEPTEMBER, 1964 AS AN
ACTION OF THE SUPREME COUNCIL OF THE
ANCIENT AND HONORABLE ORDER OF
E CLAMPUS VITUS

INDEX

* Indicates illustration.

Cain, Jessie Delilah (Dolly), 82, 105*, 183*, 189*, 193*, (see also Billeb, Mrs. Emil)
Cain, Martha Delilah Wells (Mrs. J. S.), 82, 179-180, 201, 206
Cain, Stuart Wells, 43, 57, 82, 103*, 177-178, 196, 200
Campbell, Judge, 40, 192*
Candelaria (Nevada), 1
Carson City, 36, 43-45, 50, 81, 88, 123, 170-172, 174-175
Castle Peak Mining District, 88-89, 113*
Cayhart, C. (Austin, Nevada), 13
Cease, Charlie, 131-132
Charlie (Chinese cook), 143*
China Willie, 57
Churchill County (Nev.), 15, 201
Clarke, Dr. (Tonopah), 7, 9
Cleaver, Norman, 210
Coaldale (Nevada), 3
Collins (hauling contractor), 39-40, 43-44
Copper Mountain (California), 91, 157, 159
Costello (prospector, Broken Hills), 203
Cottonwood Canyon (Calif.), 93
Cottonwood (Nevada), 16
Couch, Frank, 85
Crystal Lake (California), 89
Cunningham, Dr. J. R., 7, 9

— D —

Daniels, Mrs. (Hawthorne), 202-203, 217
Davis (prospector), 17
Dead Man Creek, Grade, 49
Death Valley Nat'l. Monument, 16
Del Monte (Nevada), 178, 180
Denham, George, 69*, 101, 200
Dennis & Warren (Tonopah), 9
Divide Mining District (Nevada), 17
Doby Jim, 128
Dodge, Ed, 22-23
Dolan, Bert (Sheriff), 84
Dolan, James P. (Sheriff), 42-43, 132-133

Dondero, John, 90
Douglas, Billy, 6
Downing, Paul M., 80
Dupuich, Dr. (Bodie), 150

— E —

Edwards, Ben, 6
Esmeralda County (Nevada), 12, 16, 86, 106
Evans, Jack, 210

— F —

Fairview (Nevada), 157
Fallon (Nevada), 15, 201
Fanger, Joe, 193*
Farrington, Walter, 75*
Fletcher Station (Nevada), 178
Forman, William, 9
Fort Churchill (Nevada), 3
Frenzel, Robert B., 210
Frisbie, Raymond D., 9

— G —

Gams, Joe, 10-11
Gardnerville (Nevada), 180
Garfield Mining District (Nev.), 47
Gilbert, Jake, 47
Glenn, Jim, 86
Gold Mountain (Nevada), 17
Golden, Frank, 6, 9
Goldfield (Nevada), 10, 14, 17-18, 32, 49-50, 32*, 86
Goldyke Mining District (Nevada), 17
Goode, Dr., 170*
Gorham, Harry, 104*
Grandpa Mining District (Nevada), 16, 32*
Green Creek Canyon, 89, 164*
Greenwater (California), 15
Gregovich, John, 9

— H —

Haggin, J. B., 78
Hamlin, R. H., 49
Hammond, Dr. (Tonopah), 7, 9, 26
Hammond, Jack 158-159

Mono Basin (California), 35, 46, 92-93, 129, 132, 157, 159, 182
Mono County (California), 23, 35, 40, 86, 92, 106, 122, 132, 135, 176, 182-183, 196, 201, 205, 208-210
Mono Craters, extinct volcanoes, 46, 70*, 133, 166*
Mono Diggings (California), 92
Mono Lake (California), 35-36, 38, 41, 45-49, 55, 69, 77, 82, 86, 91-93, 129, 132-133, 144, 146, 147* 149, 152, 155-159, 177, 190, 197, 200
Mono Mills (California), 35-36, 38-39, 42-52, 54-58, 65*-70*, 71*, 72*, 73*, 74*, 75*, 82-83, 125-132, 144*, 151, 155-159, 177, 182, 193*, 197*, 199-200, 212*-213*
Mount Brougher (Tonopah), 13, 29*, 31*
Mount Butler (Tonopah), 6, 13, 16, 26*, 29*, 30*
Mount Oddie (Tonopah), 4, 30*
Mountain House (Nevada), 180
Moyle & Gilkey, 188*
Munckton, Dr. George, 88
Murphy, Art, 186*, 187*, 193*

— N —

Nelson, "Battling", 10
Nelson (California), 4
Nelson, Joe, 4-7
Nixon, George S., 9
Nye County (Nevada), 12, 13, 17

— O —

Oakland (California), 161
Oddie, Tasker L., 9, 13
Olaqua, Frank, 189*

— P —

Paoha Island, 93*
Parker, Pat R. (Judge), 40, 182
Pat Gregory (Indian), 128
Peters, John M., 5, 7, 19-22, 49, 50, 107*
Pierce, R. T., 89
Pittman, Key, 9

— Q —

Quesso (Indian), 146*
Quong Yee, 142*
Quong Ying Lung, 143*

— R —

Rapp, Ed, 39
Rattlesnake Canyon (Nevada), 47, 50
Raycraft, J., 170*
Reading, Gould, 189*, 193*
Reading, W. E., 43
Rector, Bill, 42
Reno (Nevada), 2-3, 24*, 43, 108, 123, 152, 174-176, 180
Rhinedollar Lake (Calif.), 113*
Rhyolite (Nevada), 14, 33
Richardson, Warren, 22
Rickard, Tex, 10
Roach, Jack, 5
Robbins, Lewis, 6, 8, 22
Rosa May (Bodie), 123
Ross, Alex, 84-85
Ross, Fred, 202, 217*
Rough Creek (Springs) (California), 38, 78, 149
Rush Creek (Calif.), 156, 181, 197
Rye Patch (Nevada), 6, 21

— S —

Sacramento (California), 152
Saddleback Lake (California), 181
"Sam" ("Bad man", Bodie), 119-121, 204
Sam Leon (Bodie), 205-206
San Francisco (California), 18, 40, 45, 78, 173-176, 178-181, 199-202, 205-206, 197
Sawtooth Peak (Mount Oddie), 13
Schmidt, Kurt, 56
Schurz (Nevada), 3
Segerstrom, Donald I., 89, 203, 210
Sexton, Perry, 41-42
Sherman, Bob, 41
Sierra Nevada, 77, 88, 90-91, 135*, 153, 184*-185*, 197
Silver Lake (California), 181, 197
Silver Peak Mining District, 16

Smith, Dr. E. K., 9
Smith, F. M., "Borax King", 1
Smith, Nat, 48, 75*, 155, 158,
   186*, 187
Snyder, Charles, 88
Sodaville (Nevada), 3, 13, 24, 26,
   36, 48-50
Sonora (California), 77, 89
Southern Klondyke Mining
   District, 13, 16
Sparks (Nevada), 51
Speed, Dave, 103*, 144*
Spurr, Josiah E., 89
Stimler, Harry, 16, 18
Stinson, Ed, 65*, 87-88, 103*, 158
Sturgeon, Verna, 189*
Sweetwater (Nevada), 43, 157,
   175, 180

— T —
Thomas, Matt, 43
Thorne (Nevada), 3, 37, 151-152,
   161, 173, 179
Tim (Chinese cook, Mono Mills)
   127
Tioga Lodge (California), 200
Tonopah (Nevada), 1-33, 35-37,
   39, 48-50, 140, 171. Pictures
   24*-31*
Transvaal Mining District, 17
Tripp, Alonzo, 9
Tucker, Jim ("the Shrimp"), 6-8
Twain, Mark, 108, 110
Two Bits (Indian), 128

— V —
Vann, 217*

— W —
Wabuska (Nevada), 3
Walker, Freid, 134
Walker Lake (Nevada), 3
Ware, Dr. (Bodie), 57
Warford Springs (California), 82
Warm Springs Station
   (California), 35, 45-46, 48-49,
   93, 129, 177
Washington, George (Indian), 85
Washoe Valley (Nevada), 175
Waters (stage driver), 178
Wellington (Nevada), 43, 175, 180
Whiskey Flat (Nevada), 47, 49
White Mountains, 64*
Wilson (cowpuncher), 19
Wingfield, George, 9
Wingfield Park (Reno), 108
Wonder Mining District (Nevada),
   14, 15
Woodbury, J., 104*
Workman, prospector, 17

— Y —
Yerington (Nevada), 3, 162*
Young (hauling contractor), 39-40
Young Charlie (Indian), 128
Yribarren, John, 39-42, 193

— Z —
Zabriskie, Christian B., 1-2